DEATH WITHOUT ~~~~ICE

D1542951

Sandra Helene Straub

Death, Value and Meaning Series
Series Editor: John D. Morgan

Baywood Publishing Company, Inc.
AMITYVILLE, NEW YORK

Library of Congress Catalog Number: 99-048727
ISBN: 0-89503-214-7 (Cloth)

Library of Congress Cataloging-in-Publication Data

Straub, Sandra H., 1950-
   Death without notice / Sandra H. Straub.
       p. cm. - - (Death, value, and meaning series)
   Includes bibliographical references and index.
   ISBN 0-89503-214-7 (cloth)
   1. Sudden death- -Psychological aspects. 2. Bereavement- -Psychological aspects. 3. Grief. I. Title. II. Series.
   BF789.D4 S77 2000
   155.9'37- -dc21   99-048727

Dedication

I dedicate this book to a former instructor of mine, Mary Jane Ringkamp, retired Director of Public Relations and Education of Hospice of the South Shore, for all her special traits as a teacher. She is one of the warmest and most compassionate women I have ever met. I thank her for helping me come to terms with my grief and giving me the courage to write this book which helped to lessen the hidden guilt I had harbored inside of me for so long.

Acknowledgments

I could not have written this book without the help and support of many people.

I especially want to thank my editor, John D. Morgan for his belief in me!

I want to thank the Middle Country Public Library in Centereach, Long Island, New York, for having so many articles and books available to me for my research on the subject of death and dying. The library personnel at this branch are efficient and always willing to help.

I needed wisdom, editorial advice, and technical expertise and found exactly that from the people listed below. I thank each of you for sharing your thoughts, feelings, memories, and experiences!

Dr. Jeanne Roberts
Mary Lou Gremling
Marilyn Janson

Special gratitude goes to Mary Jane Ringkamp for her encouragement and support. The birth of this book began as a twenty-page paper submitted as a requirement in a death and dying course taught by her. The result won the Mary E. Brown Award sponsored by the Association for Death Education and Counseling.

I am grateful to my close friends who supported me in my time of grief but have since drifted away. I thank my new friends for continuing the support I so desperately needed.

I thank my daughter, Natalie, for being a big girl at such a tough time.

I thank my deceased husband, Leo, for six happy years—full of fantastic memories I will never forget.

Most of all I thank my husband, Paul, for his love and support. He truly is a very special man.

Set me a seal upon my heart, love is as strong as death.
—Viktor Frankl

Table of Contents

Preface*

Life wasn't so easy for me as a child. My parents divorced when I was two years old and while growing up I had an abusive stepfather. I was ten years old the first time I saw my biological father. He left shortly after arriving because my stepfather threatened to kill him. It was two years later that my mother divorced my stepfather because of the mental, physical, and emotional abuse he inflicted on both of us. My father returned again when I was fourteen and it was at this time my parents decided to remarry. I was the happiest child alive! It was so exciting! But ten days later my father died of a massive heart attack—my first experience with sudden death of a family member. I was devastated.

When I was eighteen, my grandmother, whom I had never met because of my parents' divorce, died just before I was to make my first visit to see her in California. My favorite aunt, at the age of thirty-three, was admitted to the hospital unexpectedly for a surgical procedure, but didn't survive the operation. A few years later my uncle, a forty-six-year-old fireman, fell from a ladder while painting and died. My niece, age twenty, was killed in a tragic automobile accident. I have had my share of sudden death.

Somehow I managed to make it through my teenage years. I married my first husband at age twenty. We were different in so many ways. Neither of us had the emotional maturity to make our marriage work. We stayed together for almost ten years before divorcing. During that time, we adopted a beautiful six-week-old Korean girl. Four years later I married Leo—an intelligent, sensitive, compassionate, and fun-loving man. It was the happiest time of my life. I not only loved him, I was "in love" with him—a feeling I had never known before. My prayers for a happy life were finally answered.

Leo died suddenly on May 12, 1984 from a brain aneurysm and it wasn't until five years later that I was able to come to terms with his death. I was constantly plagued by feelings of guilt and being totally useless. I no longer felt I had any right to exist. Every day I had to struggle to prove to myself that I was living for "something." I didn't feel capable of being loved by anyone ever again. Nothing helped.

*This book uses the personal pronoun "her" for the sake of consistency and clarity. Obviously, the experiences recounted are equally relevant to men.

Nothing mattered. I felt so confused, helpless, hopeless, lonely, and unable to face the reality of Leo's unexpected death.

In 1986, I married Paul, a wonderful and patient man. We had a great marriage but I continually compared him to Leo. Little did I know at the time how saint-like this man was and still is. It's as if God just dropped him from the sky for me—not to replace Leo, but to give me joy and a chance to live and love again.

Something was missing and I didn't know what it was. I searched for answers but couldn't find any. I realize now I just wasn't ready to accept that Leo was really gone. My grief work was not complete. I had merely put it on hold. Finally, in 1989, I decided to go back to school. I took a course called "Death and Dying" and was advised by my instructor to write Leo a letter in order to free myself from the anxiety which was overwhelming me. Maybe this letter will inspire you to write to your loved one to help you erase any guilt you may have and alleviate some of the pain deep inside. It worked for me.

The story I have to tell can happen to anyone, but the purpose of this book is to share my feelings with those of you who are suddenly alone and to express my thoughts on personal growth after the sudden death of a family member. If you have hope, happiness will come again, but you must confront the grief if you wish to recover and be a whole person again. I will support and guide you on how to handle your grief in the time of loss when you need it the most.

This book is about survival. It is for widowers as well as widows, sisters as well as brothers, mothers as well as fathers, for facing grief is not limited to one sex. I hope it can help encourage those who are suffering prolonged grief or otherwise not recovering well to get competent professional help. If you have not experienced the sudden death of a loved one, this book will help you support, inspire, and hold the hands of those who have.

I only wish to give you a glimpse of the hurt, the process, and the recovery for that is all I can give you. A walk through the ordeal of sudden death—especially in the early months—is a solitary experience. But it is one that can be hopeful, with the inspiration to move beyond loneliness and pain toward the realization that "I can live and love again."

> Sorrow comes to all . . .
> Perfect relief is not possible
> Except with time. You cannot
> Now realize that you will ever
> Feel better . . . and yet . . .
> You are sure to be happy again.
> Abraham Lincoln
> 16th President of the United States of America

November 29, 1990

Dear Leo,

It's been six years since you died but I just wanted to let you know that I still love you and miss you even though I did get married again. I laughed when you asked if I would marry again if you died and you got angry. I didn't know how serious you were and I didn't know that you were going to die two weeks later. Please forgive me. I forgive you for dying and leaving me to grieve for six long years.

I've never written a letter to a dead person before—well, according to the rest of the world, that's what you are—but in my heart you're still very much alive. I thrive on my memories of you and of all the good times we shared. Our level of affection was so intense in the five years and nine months we were together. We had extremes of love and hate, desire, happiness, and suffering. That's why this closeness we had left a big hole in my heart when you died. I ached for you constantly and at the same time felt guilt, bitterness, and resentment. I had to struggle with a new life, new problems, new relationships, new happiness, but at night in our bed, the old problems returned to haunt me. Your absence will always be present in my life. Your untimely and unnecessary death will always remain a tragedy for me. Even after all these years, from time to time something will trigger a tear. Life goes on but the unbelievable fact of your death remains.

I keep remembering the day you died in the hospital, as you lay unconscious with all those tubes coming out of you. They said you would never be the same again even if you did live—but I didn't care—my heart wanted you in any form. I never gave up. I guess things worked out for the best, Leo, because you wouldn't have wanted to live that way.

I am happy now in my new life. I'm going back to school for my nursing degree. Natalie is in the 9th grade and is a very beautiful and smart young lady—you would be proud of her. Paul is a wonderful husband and a good father and I love him very much. Before I say my final goodby, Honey, I just need you to know that I may have replaced our relationship but I did not replace you. You gave me a part of you that no one can ever take away. And no matter how many more years pass, I will treasure those memories I have of you and hold you forever close to my heart. Happy birthday, Leo! I love you and always will, and who knows, maybe we'll meet again someday.

Love always,

Sweetie Pie

Overview

Part One contains individual experiences of those who have dealt with the sudden death of a loved one. These personal vignettes introduce chapters related to specific types of deaths in the family system, such as the death of a spouse or the death of a child. It presents the three stages of grief that I personally experienced in my own grieving process. Moving through 1) numbness, 2) disorganization, and finally 3) reorganization. As a process, grief is thought of as a difficult and time-consuming procedure that must be worked through to its end. Once the stages are completed, one may be free to begin a new life. Each stage has its own tasks to complete before moving onto the next.

Part Two focuses on recovery and growth. After the stages of grief are complete, one is once again able to begin doing the things they did before their loved one's death. It outlines the journey to the beginning of a new life. It focuses on major areas of concern during grief but unknown to the griever until the stages are complete, such as shock and adjustment. It also discusses anger, guilt, anxiety, betrayal, friendship, handling the holidays, spiritual growth, and hope, as well as other areas of importance.

Part Three provides practical applications one should know—being prepared when the death of a loved one occurs. It explains the Living Will, the Durable Power of Attorney, and other legalities after a death. Facing death is something most people want to avoid. This section also provides education about death and dying. And, finally, it gives pertinent information on explaining death to a child.

Part Four offers therapeutic guidelines that can make the grief process a little easier. Grief work is an important part of the grief process. The exercises provide direct confrontation with grief and can be painful at times. It is generally a slow process and past grief may be awakened and challenged once again. It is through this pain that one grows and becomes a better person.

1

Poems and other inspirational messages are interspersed through-out the book in hope they will touch the heart and inspire a deeper commitment to oneself. They are intended to nurture the broken heart and soothe a yearning soul.

Death Without Notice offers those who are suffering a way to help prepare for the aftermath of a death. It gives hope that growth is possible once the grief process is complete. It offers courage to face inevitable challenges in a renewed life.

> To everything there is a season, and a time to every purpose under heaven:
> A time to be born, and a time to die;
> A time to plant, and a time to pluck up that which is planted . . .
> A time to weep, and a time to laugh;
> A time to mourn, and a time to dance;
> A time to get, and a time to lose;
> A time to keep, and a time to cast away;
> A time to love, and a time to hate;
> A time of war, and a time of peace . . .
>
> — Ecclesiastes 111, 1-10

Introduction

Circumstances surrounding the unexpected death of a loved one often add to the traumatic impact upon the bereaved and those left in death's wake. The impact of sudden death is devastating, for it happens without notice or a chance to anticipate what lies ahead. It allows us no time for goodbyes, no time to make amendments or to ask forgiveness for harsh words in a quarrel, and no time to declare the love we feel but rarely express verbally. This unfinished business remains unresolved. There is nothing to compare with the impact and profound shock of sudden death. It attacks the entire system—leaving it in a state of shock and disbelief. There is no preparation when sudden death occurs. The bereaved are left with a sense of unreality that may last a long time. They have a stronger than normal sense of guilt. The need to blame someone for what has happened is uncontrollable. It elicits a sense of helplessness and hopelessness on the part of the survivor. There is a stronger need to know why it happened which generally leads one to blame God.

This book was written to help the bereaved gain the necessary knowledge and skills to move effectively through their grief. When someone you love dies, the pain and fear wash over you in waves. You may feel that you simply cannot bear it. You wonder if you will survive. It is true that almost everything will change. You will remember and grieve a little all the rest of your life. From my own experience, however, I can tell you that you have more strength than you realize. You *can* get through this sadness. I believe this book can help you. No one can tell you how long or in what manner you should grieve since your grief is unique from anyone else who has suffered the sudden loss of a loved one. But there are components of bereavement that are common to all of us who pass through it. Understanding these common bonds and how others have dealt with them can be of great help.

The death of a loved family member or friend brings a flood of feelings—sorrow, loneliness, abandonment, anger, and guilt. These feelings make the task of mourning one of our most painful human experiences. In this book we will examine the grief you are feeling, help you to understand what it means to mourn, and suggest some ways you can face the task of grieving. You will be provided with very practical advice that can be quickly put to work: specific solutions to the difficulties confronting survivors and personal stories from others who not only endured but became stronger individuals. Make the journey, then, with courage and with faith. Believe that as demanding and frightening as it may be, grief will become joy once more, and the love that was lost will reappear in deeper and more meaningful ways. Only by fully living through the darkness can we find our lives again, not just as they were—for they will never again be the same—but enriched by this fierce and lonely passage.

This book is about hope and personal growth after the sudden loss of a loved one. There is no magic wand to wave or healing potion to take to erase the pain. At a time of loss, survivors need guidance and support. Here is a book that offers it—to widows and widowers, to sisters and brothers, to parents and children, to friends, and to those anxious to help them.

The soul would have no rainbow if the eyes had no tears.
— Author Unknown

PART ONE

Encountering the Sudden Death of Loved Ones

CHAPTER 1

Sudden Death

Sudden deaths are those that occur without notice. When death occurs with little or no warning, and especially if it occurs in the younger years, then an extra parameter is added. There has been no opportunity for preparation beforehand. The death brings an extra effect of shock over and above the normal. When we know a death is coming we can make the necessary arrangements. We can write wills, settle financial debts, plan a funeral, contact relatives, and even say goodbye to our dying loved one. Although expected death brings shock and disbelief, we can bring some order to the chaos that accompanies it. But an unexpected death is even more shocking and more difficult to cope with. We are unprepared emotionally. The shock effect of sudden death may be so great that it causes post-traumatic stress syndrome in the bereaved. The event of the death or the circumstances under which news of the death was received may be so stressful that it overwhelms the survivor. Traumatic memories of the event preoccupy and intrude upon the mind of the bereaved often causing nightmares and psychological complications.

Sudden death is unnatural. It destroys our sense of control. It leaves us struggling for answers which may never come. We ask "Why?" over and over again. There is an increased need to understand when any death occurs but, in the case of sudden death, there is an even stronger interest—especially when a death has been traumatic. Along with this is the need to attribute not only the cause but the blame. At this point, God often becomes the only available target for one's recriminations, and it is not uncommon to hear someone say "I hate God" when they are struggling to find answers and put the pieces together following a death.

The circumstances of unexpected death may be filled with violence or there may be a sudden collapse with desperate and unsuccessful attempts at resuscitation. The bereaved may be present at the time the death occurred and helpless in preventing it. If away from the scene, the bereaved may have difficulty comprehending the death as a reality because they last saw their loved one healthy and alive.

Categorizing sudden deaths is a difficult task. While deaths from accidents, murders, and disasters are unexpected, that doesn't mean they are necessarily uncommon. Accidents are a leading cause of death—especially of young people. To pick up the newspaper and read about another automobile accident that has claimed the life of one or more people is a common occurrence in our daily lives. Accidental deaths are extremely frequent in many Western societies. No comfort exists in the idea that accidents are common. They are still unexpected and they attack the course of our lives. We are stunned, shocked, and totally unprepared.

While automobile, swimming, or other sporting event accidents shock us as human beings, some accidents paralyze us because of the number of people who have died. These incomprehensible deaths include those caused by airline crashes, hurricanes, floods, earthquakes, fires, wars, and terrorist attacks. It is far more difficult for us to understand the deaths of a large number of people at once—to grasp the loss of an entire building containing people.

Violent deaths involving murder is one area of unexpected death that is very frightening to us. Experts in law enforcement tell us that the nature of murder has changed over the years. Murder was once a much more personal affair than it appears to be now. The victims often knew the person who killed them. Murders were considered "crimes of passion." Now, however, murders are happening between people unknown to each other. Again, when you pick up the newspaper, it is not unheard of to read that some person has been killed in an act of random violence or by the hands of a serial killer. The violence of these deaths compounds the trauma and shock effects of sudden death and these responses are difficult to resolve. The shock of the death is complicated by hatred for the killer. Violent and accidental deaths are all the more shocking, abnormal, and difficult to understand when they involve children. Gangs drive by in violent rampages and shoot a child on a bicycle. This kind of murder frightens and threatens our understanding of the world we live in.

Then we have suicide. Suicide has been a concern of humanity throughout history. Our many cultures respond to suicide in different ways. Some react with horror and disdain while others display honor and pride. Suicides are deaths with special significance. Here the person has chosen to die, to desert those who love them. These deaths may be violent, as with shooting, stabbing, or hanging. Or they may be quiet as with sleeping pills. The result is uncertainty, blame, guilt, and hostility for the bereaved.

Unique to sudden death is the sense of helplessness that it elicits on the part of the survivor. This type of death is an assault on our sense of power and on our sense of orderliness. This is often linked with an incredible sense of rage and causes the bereaved person to want to vent anger on someone—again, in many cases, God.

Unfinished business is more of a concern of sudden deaths than slow deaths. As in all deaths, there are many regrets for things the bereaved did not say and things they never got around to doing with or for the deceased. However, when a death occurs unexpectedly, the opportunity to resolve these issues is no longer there. Counseling can help the bereaved to deal with these unresolved issues and find some way to closure.

Death

The winds of time blow through the trees
With many melodies;
Melodies of life's little tragedies.
Is death a tragedy or a melody?
This your mind must listen to in your memory
What will it be?
The path is up to thee.

– Joseph Contento

COMPLICATIONS AFTER A SUDDEN DEATH

Death without notice creates special problems for survivors. The suddenness of the death alone is overpowering. There is no time to anticipate and prepare for the loss. The survivor's coping abilities are attacked by the sudden and dramatic knowledge of the death. The aftermath of sudden, unanticipated loss tends to leave the loved one in a state of shock—stunned, feeling out of control, and confused. They are unable to grasp the reality of what has happened. It is unbelievable and incomprehensible. The shock of the death affects the survivor both emotionally and physically and persists for an extended period of time.

The survivors of sudden death go through the grief process just as other mourners do, but the devastating effects of the shock tend to compromise their completion. Their grief is often intensified. They become helpless and hopeless. The capacity to cope diminishes. The world they live in is totally shattered without warning. What was once a safe and orderly world has now become one which is insecure and unpredictable. The death does not make sense and cannot be understood. There was no closure—no chance to say goodby and deal with unfinished business. Death without notice causes more intense emotional reactions, such as anger, guilt, anxiety, vulnerability, confusion, and disorganization. As a result of these emotions, the bereaved become obsessed with the deceased. There is a need to find meaning in the death and to determine who is responsible for causing it. And last but not least, the death tends to be followed by many secondary losses—loss of home, identity, financial status, future plans, goals, dreams, and self.

> No thing, is a hard thing to look at.
> But something, that was there, still is!
> — Author Unknown

DEATH IN THE FAMILY SYSTEM

Our first experiences with death are frequently with a family member—one of our grandparents, sisters, brothers, parents, or the family pet. The response of our family to death is where our values first begin to form regarding death and dying. Can the topic of death be raised in our family? Is death something to be feared? Will our fears be laughed at? The answer to these questions will depend on how each of us learned about death and dying. The willingness to talk about death in the family is a major shift in attitude in modern American society. Children of today have grown up with a more open attitude to a number of sensitive topics. It is no longer unthinkable to talk about funeral arrangements with aging parents, with dying spouses, siblings, or even with a close friend. The family begins our understanding of death and dying.

To encounter death in the family means to face the reality that our loved ones will someday die. The attitude of the past has been that this idea is too painful to face and should not be talked about. The inclusion of death and dying as one more area of life which can be openly talked about holds a promise—that the isolated, lonely and frightening death of family members is of the past. Encountering death in the family becomes important as one more way to insure that our fears, doubts, and questions do not result in relationships in which our love and compassion are not expressed.

Leo

Have you ever had a rug pulled out from under your feet? That's what the sudden death of a spouse is like. One minute you're together and laughing—the next minute you're alone and crying. After being previously married for ten years and divorced, I wanted to make sure everything would work out the next time around. Leo and I lived together for four years before getting married on August 20, 1982. Our married life together lasted for only one year and nine months.

Day 1 – Saturday, May 12, 1984, 12:30 A.M.

Leo and I came home from our bowling league, had a snack, and went to bed. You've often heard people say "Oh, what a way to go" or "When I die, I want to die in bed making love," but you never really expect it to happen that way. You expect it to happen that way only in the movies—but not this night. Just as Leo climaxed, he collapsed on top of me with grunting sounds coming from his throat. Somehow I managed to turn the light on. What I saw were the whites of his eyes and a twitching of his eyelids. I didn't know what had happened. He wasn't responding to my voice or my touch. I worked my way out from underneath his 205 pounds, checked his pulse, but found nothing, and then immediately dialed 911. The ambulance came and took him to the hospital. Sometime later the doctor came out and told me that Leo had an aneurysm—something I had never heard of before—and that medication would be administered to bring down the swelling in his brain. I knew then this was a serious matter. Oh God, not his brain! That's all I could say. I couldn't believe what was happening! It had to be a nightmare!

> The first response to the news of the death of a loved one is one of shock, numbness, and disbelief. The bereaved person feels a sense of unreality, as though what has been said or what has happened could not possibly be true—as though it could not have been said, as though it must be happening to someone else. The bereaved may feel distanced from the horror and its implications, frozen in time. There is a feeling of being in a dream or a nightmare from which she will awake (Raphael, 1983, p. 34).

When I left St. Charles Hospital that morning at 3:00 A.M., Leo was 97 percent brain dead. Of all the bad things that had happened to me since my childhood, I feel this was absolutely the worst.

Day 2 – Sunday, May 13, 1984 (Mother's Day)

The nightmare continues. As if I had not gone through enough already, I now had to watch Leo die, lying in that hospital bed on a respirator, with all those tubes and bottles connected to him.

> When death is not instantaneous, extensive technological attempts to save the victim's life may also profoundly affect the dying and those who will be bereaved. Intensive care and resuscitation are vital attempts to prevent untimely deaths and are, of course, frequently successful. When they fail, however, the dying takes on a special aura, for the dying person may seem distanced and dehumanized by the tubes and machines, by the drips and the respirators. These resuscitative attempts are critical of course for both the dying and those who will be bereaved, but their psychological and social relevance must be recognized for it is often a constraint upon the individuals and family unit (Raphael, 1983, p. 29).

It was so hard to handle—to see him like that. It wasn't the Leo I knew. I had so much love for him. He had to be comforted. Although he was unconscious, I somehow hoped that he knew I was there. I sat by his bed and held his hand and begged him to wake up. I bought him cards and puzzle books even though I knew his brain wasn't functioning. Maybe, just maybe, the doctors were wrong. I was in denial.

Day 3 – Monday, May 14, 1984, 10:00 A.M.

After three days of CAT scans, I had a decision to make: leave Leo on the respirator for the rest of his so-called life or turn the respirator off and let him die. What a decision! Which would it be? I decided that it wasn't fair for me or my eight-year-old daughter to see him like this every day. I knew Leo would not have wanted it this way either. My mother-in-law wanted her son to remain on the respirator, but the doctor told me it was my decision. Knowing that Leo was brain dead and would never return to normal, I knew what I had to do. After I gave permission to unplug the machine, my mother-in-law screamed and called me a murderess. Maybe I had made a mistake. I wasn't thinking of her feelings. I was so confused! I didn't want to live anymore because I couldn't face what was happening to my life. Leo died twenty-six hours after they pulled the plug—after each of his major organs had failed. My head was on his chest when his heart stopped beating. At that moment I lost my husband, my lover, and my best friend.

I went home and took some pills and then I took more. I eventually took every pill I could find in my medicine cabinet and became very sick. Friends who were staying at my house took me back to the hospital sometime later that morning; I had my stomach pumped—or whatever they do to keep you alive. I didn't know if I really wanted to kill myself—I just wanted to numb the pain. There was no one for me to talk to.

Day 4 – Tuesday, May 15, 1984

An autopsy was performed to determine the cause of death. It was this day that I told Natalie her daddy had died and would never come home again. I really don't remember exactly what I said; however, I do remember asking her if she wanted to attend the funeral and she replied with a definite, "No." I am sure her refusal occurred because I had taken her to the hospital to visit Leo. She reacted hysterically when she saw him connected to the respirator. I tried to encourage her to attend the funeral—thinking that she may regret it later—but, she kept refusing so I did not force her to go.

Day 5 – Wednesday, May 16, 1984

Now the Wake. When would it ever end? The days of Hell go on and on. I was given a sedative, but without my family and friends with me, I would not have survived. Friends and relatives from all over came to pay their respects. There were so many flowers the funeral home had to use an additional room just to hold them. I don't know how I did it. My sisters stood by me and practically dared his family to approach me—especially after what was said to me at the hospital.

Day 6 – Thursday, May 17, 1984

The Funeral. It was a beautiful spring day—flowers blooming, birds chirping—but Leo was dead. I had nothing to feel happy about. How could this be? He was only thirty-one years old! He loved life far too much to leave it. It just wasn't fair!

Now that the six days of Hell were over, I still had to tolerate telephone hang ups and threats. His family wanted his belongings. I purchased an answering machine and that helped tremendously. I kept the volume down low and had my friends listen to the messages. They screened each and every call, keeping only the messages that had nothing to do with Leo's family. I thought it was over, but the grief was there every day to remind me of what I had gone through.

For a while I felt as if I were on the outside looking in at myself. In the days that followed I tried not to think; however, I still had to do all those necessary things. I kept busy—the lawyer, the bank, answering all those cards and letters, the telephone calls. I tried to force a smile. I had no feelings and can remember absolutely nothing of what I did for the first year following Leo's death. I was numb. The silence at home was awful. I would call his name, hoping he would answer or imagine the key in the lock when I expected him home from work. Our dog sat by the door daily waiting for Leo to return.

> People in shock sometimes look stoical, as if they are coping without much emotion. The truth is that in shock we do not feel the full impact of loss and therefore we are not yet suffering as we will once the numbness wears off. Observing someone who is in great pain acting in a stoical, seemingly unemotional way can be a bewildering experience. But this apparent stoicism is actually a robotlike way of functioning. To be able to function at all may reassure us that we are coping and not falling apart at the impact of our loss (Tatelbaum, 1984, p. 26).

Sometimes in the middle of conversations I would suddenly leave—find some place to cry. It seemed all I ever did was cry, but never in front of anyone. I had to be brave. I had so much tension inside of me. The pain was unbearable.

> It is natural now for us to weep a great deal. Tears are nature's way of helping us express and release our pain. We may ruminate over and be intensely preoccupied with the details of the lost loved one's life or death, over our relationship with one another, over our memories, over our last encounter, and over unfinished business together, or even over our more abstract ideas about death. So bewildered are we by the fact of death that many of us become preoccupied for a time with deep questions about *why* the loved one died (Tatelbaum, 1984, p. 28).

I had trouble breathing. I didn't know where the pain was—my chest or my heart. My stomach ached. My head ached. I felt tired all the time. I had no energy to get out of bed. I had a lack of interest in everything.

> Bewilderment and despair often continued beyond the first impact of loss. There were still periods of weeping, although widowers were more apt than widows to feel choked up rather than to express themselves through tears. Many physical symptoms appeared and sometimes lingered for weeks or months. Aches and pains, poor

appetite, loss of stamina, headaches, dizziness, and menstrual irregularities were reported by many. Sleep disturbances were especially common and distressful. A widow would go to bed hoping to forget her cares for a while and to wake up the next morning with more energy and a brighter outlook. Often, however, she would wake up instead in the middle of the night and remain tormented by grief and the reality of the partner's absence (Kastenbaum, 1986, p. 326).

I tried not to think of Leo because it hurt so much, but as the days went by I found myself thinking of all the special things he did and said to me. The nicknames Leo gave to me like "Sweetie Pie" and "Sweet Cheeks" kept coming into my mind. The motorcycle trips we made, the sports we loved and were involved in, and the games we played to prove we were smarter than the other. I missed these things so much.

Frequently, the widows were immersed in memories of their husbands. These were usually comforting thoughts. Although, it remained painful to review the events leading up to the death, memories of the husband himself and of shared experiences generally were positive (Kastenbaum, p. 1986, p. 328).

Two weeks after Leo's death I found out I was six weeks pregnant. This was a result of three trips to Norfolk, Virginia where I had *in vitro* fertilization due to an infertility problem on my part. One month later I had a miscarriage. I guess it was fate—just another constant reminder of Leo's death had the baby lived.

I tried to sleep in our bed where *it* happened but the tears would not let me rest. I tossed and turned night after night. I was tired, exhausted, and forever crying. I would imagine Leo next to me and then realize it wasn't true. Then the dreams came—or the nightmares, I should say. I would hear Leo calling my name and when I sat up in my bed he would be standing in the doorway with his hands outstretched motioning for me to come. There was a twisted, evil smile on his face. The worse nightmare of all was the rapping at my window. I would get up and go to the window to see what the noise was and there I would see Leo's body, deteriorating, his hands clawing at the window, his face sunken in with rotting flesh and tears coming down his face. These nightmares went on for about three weeks. I was afraid to go to sleep for fear of dreaming.

Dreaming may also be affected during the mourning period. Dreams are a major means of re-experiencing and working through emotionally charged experiences and of problem-solving. Much

> grief work gets done in our sleep. Unpleasant dreams or night-
> mares may occur at any time in our lives, but they may be more
> memorable or more disturbing when we are grieving and vul-
> nerable (Tatelbaum, 1984, p. 31).

I tried to replace those dreams with good dreams, but I couldn't.
I could not visualize his face the way I remembered him before he
died. I could see the shape of his body and then even that would fade
away. I could not even remember the sound of his voice! I stared at his
picture, smiled at memories and imagined him with me. I did this for
hours in the day just to keep his image alive.

The physical side of bereavement was horrible. I felt torn apart.
Nothing helped. Some days I felt like I was able to function but only as
if I were a machine you could turn on and off. I was alive—or at least I
existed. I didn't like anything—my daughter, friends, music, food—
nothing. My daughter was keeping me alive so I disliked her the most.
I couldn't kill myself, although I eventually did make a small attempt
at it once again—subconsciously, I suppose. My daughter needed me
and, besides, Leo would be angry with me if I had taken my own life.

> Flirtations with self-destruction were not unusual. Three weeks
> after their husband's death twenty percent of a sample said they
> would welcome death if it were not for their children, and another
> six percent said they would simply welcome death, without qualifi-
> cation (Glick, 1974, p. 63).

I had to do something. I had to stop feeling sorry for myself. I went
to the library and checked out every book on grief. I felt all alone. I
couldn't share any of my feelings, unless it was with someone who had
gone through the same thing. No one understood. They all said they
did—but how could they? I still had trouble sleeping. I wanted so badly
to turn back the clock. I hated my life. I couldn't socialize with the same
friends anymore. There were just too many memories. I did manage to
make new friends—people who never knew Leo. I eventually began
going to parties and pretending to be fine when inside I was a bundle of
nerves. It was strange going to parties without Leo and not standing by
his side. People kept saying, "It will get better." How the hell did they
know?! They had no way of knowing how I felt. All I wanted was to have
Leo back. Nothing else mattered. This may seem strange, but my grief
kept me close to him—the terrible longing for him and the agony of his
death kept him on my mind. I didn't want to take a shower after he died
because he was all over me and in me. For days I kept wearing the

same clothes because Leo's smell was on them. Leo loved my feet so I kept looking at them. I really thought I was going crazy! How I functioned is still beyond me.

I met Paul one month after Leo died and I must say he was my savior—the best thing that could have ever happened to me since Leo's death. He saved my life, he saved me, but something was different. Grief changed me. I just wasn't the same person anymore and never would be. I had been through too much.

> The secret ingredient of identity reformulation is for a widow to establish new relationships, not as a substitute for her past marriage identity, but as a satisfying present endeavor that will permit her to see—and leave—her past in the past. Moreover, it will give her an updated, revised reflection of who she is. Having evolved a new definition of her self, she will be able to grow beyond widowhood (DiGiulio, 1989, p. 51).

Most of my religious beliefs have been destroyed due to previous childhood experiences and the death of many of my relatives. I don't know if I believe in Heaven, but I do believe Leos' spirit is somewhere. The thought that he was waiting for me drew me to thoughts of suicide. Even though I wanted to die, a part of me realized that I still had a daughter who needed me even if life without Leo was unbearable. I have come a long way since then. I can talk about him and the good times, laugh at the memories and smile when someone mentions his name. It's when I am weak—feeling down or just moody—that I cry. I feel I overcame my grief faster than others—maybe too fast—because I accepted invitations and listened to suggestions—I had to or I would not have survived. Actually, I believe I tried too hard the first few years to get through my grief—to have it over and done with. It wasn't until I wrote a letter to Leo that I felt a cleansing take place throughout my soul. I felt as if I were really making headway toward a new beginning. A change came over me.

Death–A New Beginning

> Death is like going from winter to spring or summer to fall and then back again. It is similar to when a caterpillar becomes a beautiful butterfly and flies away into the warm sunlight. It is like a flower that wilts away only to bloom again the following year. It is much like the last leaf that drops from a tree in the fall only to sprout again in the spring. It is like a snake that sheds its skin or a snail

that changes its shell to find a new home. It is like when the sun goes down and the moon comes out to give us a different kind of light. It is like leaving your mother's womb to enter a strange and new home. Or like leaving our present world to exist in a new place. It is a new beginning.

Sandi Straub
October, 1994

I think my biggest problem now, after six years, is that I know how hard I worked to bear the pain and survive through it all and now I feel guilty because I did. I'm afraid that if I don't think about Leo or cry about what happened—not just for him but for all my other relatives who have died—he will slip totally away from me. I want to keep his memory alive. I know I am not alone. Death ends a life but it does not end a relationship. I have a new life now, but Leo will forever be in my heart.

I did a lot of research to try and understand why I was feeling the way I did. I wanted to know how long it would take for me to recover from my grief. I now know each of us experiences the death of someone we love in our own unique way. I combined several of the theories I researched and developed stages to describe my own personal reactions and feelings. Whatever you are feeling, your response is right for you. Leo's body was buried but the emotions I felt for him continue to survive.

The story of Leo's death (taken from my personal journal) was first written in 1989 when I took a college course in death and dying. This paper won the Mary E. Brown Award presented by the Association for Death Education and Counseling. In 1990, after some encouragement from my instructor, I attempted to expand the paper into a book. It was not an easy task. I would write and sob and sob some more. It seemed I was crying more than writing so I put the book away for another seven years. After receiving my doctorate in 1997, I devoted most of my time to completing this book. I realize now the pain and tears were all part of my grief work.

Writing this book has helped me to alleviate the bitterness and guilt I had been harboring inside for so long. I always wondered how long it would be before I was freed from the pain of Leo's death. I don't think that will ever completely happen for the scars will always be there. I know now that death is a fact of life and there is just nothing one can do about it, but accept it. I remember something C. S. Lewis said: "Grief is like a bomber circling around and dropping its bombs each time the circle brings it overhead." How true! The grief just keeps coming back.

The Serenity Prayer

God grant me the serenity
to accept the things I cannot change,
courage to change the things I can,
and the wisdom to know the difference.

Living one day at a time,
enjoying one moment at a time,
accepting hardship as the pathway to peace.

Taking, as He did, this world as it is,
not as I would have it;
trusting that He will make all things
right if I surrender to His will;

That I may be reasonably happy in this life,
and supremely happy with Him forever in the next.
— Reinhold, 1934, p. 267
Excerpt from *Death & Dying, Life & Living*

WHEN A SPOUSE DIES

Diane

We were in the process of moving to a new home. I had a new job. My daughter had just finished a difficult pregnancy and my wife spent much of her time with my daughter. She discovered she had breast cancer, and had decided on a mastectomy. She had always been afraid of cancer.

We were home together almost by chance. I had a doctor's appointment scheduled so we were alone in our house. I would run home Saturday night and return for her operation on Monday. When we awoke in the morning, she turned to me and we made love. It had been an infrequent occurrence the last couple of years, and she surprised me by instigating it. Afterwards she got up to use the bathroom. When she came back, I remembered being surprised that she made no attempt to put her pajamas back on. As I watched, she made a gurgling sound and her eyes rolled back in her head. I knew that she was dead in that instant, but I called emergency 911 and the EMT squad responded quickly. But I knew. When we got to the hospital one of the first doctors there was our regular physician who was shocked. He had just examined her.

— Thomas M. Craig

John

John and I met in June of 1970. I was just out of my sophomore year in high school. John was about to enter his senior year. That winter we became engaged. We were married in September of 1974.

About a year before the birth of our first child, John started to drive a truck. An 18 wheeler, as some know it. One day he asked me to go with him on that day's load. I had gone many times and always enjoyed the time with him. On this occasion, though, I declined . . . telling John that I just did not feel right about going that day. On the way home that evening, John was passing a motor home. It was hot and all the windows were open. While passing the vehicle, the motor home crossed the center line hitting John's truck on the right-hand side. All the mirrors, and part of the window were broken, and the glass was all over the passenger side. If I had gone with him, I would surely have been badly cut by the glass. It soon became apparent to John and myself, and others at his place of work, that I had been given a gift from God. Whenever the group convoyed they always asked how I felt about the trip. I never knew what was going to happen, but I would start crying, and tell John to take extra care. Things like whiteouts, deer, and cars cutting them off happened on those occasions.

About two months after our second child was born, John was in a horrible accident. He was driving a tanker truck, empty. When he rounded a sharp curve, he saw, too late, that there was a car straddling the fog line. He had no choice, and no chance to react. He ran right over the top of the car. The truck was thrown over the edge of the road straight into a group of trees. At the last minute, the truck and trailer did a 180-degree turn. The trailer hit the trees and caught fire. If the truck had hit first, John would have been crushed by the weight of the trailer. There was no one in the car. It had run out of gas. Another tanker behind John was able to put out the fire. When John returned home, we had a long talk. We firmly believed that God had saved John's life—that John had a destiny to fulfill, and he had not yet accomplished it. Shortly thereafter, I became pregnant. Not a planned pregnancy . . . a gift from God. Once more John and I talked. We both came to the conclusion that his destiny had been fulfilled, and that John's future was up to him. That although God was watching over us . . . John could not tempt fate again.

Then, on July 20, 1984, once again I got that horrible feeling. John and I said goodbye at the front door at about 2:30 A.M. I cried. I tried so hard not to let John see how devastated I was. I told him I loved him, and to take care, and then I pushed him out the door. I watched his tail lights go down the road and around the corner. I wanted to go after him and tell him NOT to go. But I had three small children in bed. I thought about getting them up. I considered just leaving them home alone. I had to stop John. I thought about calling the shop, but the phone would ring in the boss' house, and I did not want to wake him up. Then I realized that I was paralyzed, totally unable to even pick up a foot. The whole time I was considering all my options for contacting John, I was paralyzed. As soon as I decided that I was unable to stop him, and placed him in God's hands I was able to move. I took this as a sign from God that I was not to become involved, and that He had control of everything. I put my trust and faith in God.

At 5:15 A.M., I was awakened by John yelling, "Oh God!" There was a loud clap of thunder and a torrential downpour began. I remember crying out, "Oh, John!" and slumping back down into bed. I got up at my usual time and did my usual things with the kids. Then, at about 1:15 P.M., the phone rang. The person on the other end said she was calling from the hospital in Redding, California—that she had news of my husband. I said, "He's dead, isn't he?" Her reply was, "Yes, Ma'am, he is." I have never felt such pain. I later found out that John died sometime around 5:15 A.M.

I blamed God for killing John. I ranted, raved, swore, and hated God for killing John. For a long time I prayed to God to explain Himself. How could He take John and expect me to raise three young children? I was only thirty, and they were two, four, and six years old. People at church tried to comfort me, to no avail. Then, as time went on, I started to accept my fate. I learned to accept the fact that God does not kill. He may allow a death to happen, but He does not kill. I did, however, continue to pray to God for an answer as to why.

Then, one night, I had a vision. God was giving me my answer. I saw John and our three children in a car. They were traveling on a road about a mile from our house. I saw another car run a stop sign and hit our car. I saw John, my daughter, and my sons . . . dead. All dead. I was totally alone. Then God spoke to me in my vision. He told me that He knew that John was going to die soon. He allowed John to die that day in the truck, because if He hadn't, John would have died very soon taking all three of our children with him. I was given the gift of my childrens' lives.

I am still upset that John died. I missed him. More than a heart could ever express. But I have three happy, healthy children now almost fully grown. My daughter is attending college, hopefully getting a teaching degree. My eldest son has graduated high school, and plans on attending college and getting a degree in Vascular Technology. My youngest is still in high school and taking some college courses. I love and appreciate all three of my gifts from God.

— Janet Hottman

Len

I lost my first husband when I was thirty-nine years old. He also was thirty-nine. We had been married for nineteen and a half years and had a good marriage. Oh, we had our normal problems, but all and all it was a good marriage, and we were happy. We had four daughters and life seemed good. Never in my wildest dreams did I think or know that life at that time was about to change forever.

On a warm, foggy February night, my husband was not feeling well. He thought he had indigestion. So did I. I was at work that night and my oldest daughter, seventeen at the time, came to work to get me. She said, "Mom, Dad doesn't look good. You better come home and check on him." When I got home, he said it was just indigestion, and he was feeling better. I asked if he wanted to go to the emergency ward and get checked out because he did have high blood pressure. But he said no, and for me to go back to work—that he was okay. When I got home that night, he met me by the back door, and he seemed fine. Now looking back, I can see that he didn't look fine, but at the time, it seemed he did. We went to bed, and he just could not sleep. He got up and said he thought he had to use the bathroom. That was the last thing he ever said to me. He had a myocardial infarction, which means heart attack. He lived long enough to get a pacemaker put in, but he had no brain waves, and he died. And, I died too.

I remember thinking on the way to the hospital, as the rescue workers were fighting to save his life, that this is a nightmare. I am going to wake up and find out that I am dreaming all of this. At the same time, I knew that he was gone from me forever. I kept saying I wanted a priest to give him last rights as soon as we got to the hospital. This was done, and it was that priest that came out and tried to prepare me for what he knew the doctors were about to tell me. Your husband is dead. I did not hear anything. I saw his mouth moving, but I was somewhere else. I remember being taken in to see him and thinking this is not real. He looks like he is sleeping. He is going to get up. The next thing I knew a nurse opened my hand and slapped the ring into it. That was it. I was no longer married to the man on the table. I know now that it was for my protection, so that the ring would remain safe, but at the time, I felt like she was saying to me—it's over. I remember wanting to run out of the hospital and just start screaming and running. People were around me asking all kinds of questions, and I had to answer them. This is no time to ask a new widow questions. The law should be changed. There has to be another way.

The three oldest girls knew that their dad was gone. They all were at the hospital. My seven-year-old was with neighbors and had no idea. My brother drove me home, and I remember thinking that the house did not look the same to me as we pulled up the side drive. It was my house, but it had a strange look to it. That is a hard feeling to describe. I also felt like I was lopsided. Like half of my body was missing. Most of that night is still a blank. I cannot to this day put all of it together. I remember some of the people that were over, but not all. When the little one came home, I told her that dad was in heaven, and I remember telling her he was gone, but cannot remember just how I told her. I may never remember that. I was like a robot, just doing things and not even really knowing how I was doing it all. I started sobbing and crying at the hospital and don't think I stopped for a good six months. This is no exaggeration. I used to think to myself that all of my tears could have made a new lake or a good size river. For the next week, I was surrounded by people from all over. The shock of my husband's death, since he was so young, affected everyone. No one could believe it. The kids seemed to be okay and I remember being angry at them because they did not seem to be as upset as I thought they should be. They were, but, at the time, I felt different. We got through the funeral and the paperwork and, after about a month, life went on for everyone else but me. The kids had their friends and seemed to be getting along. All but two of my friends, Sarah and Joanne, dumped me. Some I have never heard from again and it's been seventeen years. This happens. The kids did not talk about anything. Whatever they were feeling was in them and not being told to me. I was too grief stricken to find out. Life, as far as I was concerned, had come to an end. Nothing mattered anymore. I felt betrayal on his part. I hated anyone old. They should be dead—not him. I had to stop going to church for a long time because I was angry at God. I felt isolated and alone. I have no idea how the heck I got through that first year. The void was overwhelming. Little by little, I did recover. I spent months in my room. My oldest girls took care of the little one. I sort of stopped everything. I started to drink more than I should and life became out of control. I was used and abused by men, and I let it happen because I needed to feel loved. I stopped eating and drank so much that I got sick. I could not sit in my living room for a year. I could not clear out any of his things for about two years. I could not listen to tapes with his voice on it for about four years. I could not remove the knife from my heart for about three years. I lived with the feeling that I had somehow done something wrong, and God was paying me back. I was lost.

Thank God, after about three years, I was able to pull myself together. At about five years, I had recovered enough to feel good again. I do not hurt over this death anymore. After seventeen years, the pain is gone. I have never forgotten my first husband. He is in my heart and always will be. The memories are as bright as ever, and I smile and laugh when I think of him. I was able to take him out of my present life and put him in that special place in my heart that no one can ever take him out of. He is resting in peace, and I have resolved his loss.

— Rose Mahan

*　　*　　*

What is a widow? What is a widower? The dictionary defines them as a person whose spouse has died and who has not remarried. One never expects to grow up and be a widow or a widower. One assumes that the family will always be intact, that no one important will die, that living a good life will be rewarded, and that life is fair. Then sudden death occurs and changes the way the wife or husband views their world. The surviving spouse must now stop including their loved one in future plans, thoughts, and conversations. Being widowed was not easy. It was probably the most difficult challenge of my life. Being alone with a slew of additional responsibilities was frustrating and overwhelming. Being both mother and father to my daughter was almost more than I could bear. Not only had I lost Leo, but everything about my life from that point on changed forever. I lost the economic security provided by a two-income household, a wonderful marriage, a great friendship, sharing in the raising of our daughter, and growing old together.

One feels totally helpless when death strikes their spouse. There are so many questions and so few answers—if any. This chapter does not try to solve the problems that you face as a widow or widower, but it attempts to deal with the central issues that are present in your life after the death of your spouse. It is intended to provide support in your suffering and to make you aware that you are not isolated in what you are feeling. It will help you go through the pain of the death and find a new life. Right now, all you may want to do is run from the pain and avoid the grief of your situation—to bury your feelings rather than have others see you crying or depressed. This only leads to prolonged grief, as well as physical and emotional illness. Going through the grief rather than steering clear of the agony will eventually help you find a new beginning in life. By dealing primarily with feelings common to men and women, this chapter is intended for both widows and widowers. Its aim is to be a spiritual and an emotional support. As an individual, you can use it for personal healing; as a member of a support group, you can utilize it as a resource to share in your discussions; and as a professional, you can gain the necessary knowledge and skills to work effectively with the bereaved spouse, both individually and in groups.

On your journey through grief, there are several things you can do to help yourself: accept the reality, express your emotions, and find support in others.

Facing the finality of death brings on an emotional tidal wave. You have never been more alone than at the time of the announcement of your spouse's death. The words hit you like a ton of bricks. With the pain in your head, your heart, and your soul—you are lucky to be alive yourself.

Although you try to fight the finality of death's call, the funeral arrangements need to be made. You need to contact a funeral director, choose a coffin, purchase a cemetery plot, pick out flowers, plan the wake, select clothes for the body, print the death notice, inform relatives and friends, decide on the church service and eulogy, and make the lodging arrangements for and await the arrival of long-distance family members and friends. In addition, plans need to be made for the closing of the coffin, funeral procession, hearses, pallbearers, the cemetery, the meal after the funeral, and thank you cards. There are more decisions to make in half a day than you are expected to make in a year. You finally realize this is not a bad dream. It is reality. Your spouse is dead.

Each death is unique. Everyone expresses his or her emotions to life's greatest hurts differently. Some cry uncontrollably while others become extremely sullen. You may constantly question "Why?" or you may totally withdraw from others. You were emotionally wounded. It is natural to feel this way, but you must express your emotions in order to heal. Where, when, and how often is up to you for everyone is different and there are no set rules in dealing with death.

Don't put additional pressure on yourself by thinking you have to always be strong and not break down for the sake of the children or other family members. Depend on others to help. Cry when the need arises. You don't have to be strong all of the time. Do not be afraid to mourn openly.

Many times there will be no one around with whom to share your feelings. And, when there is, you may not feel like talking. Keep a journal. Write down your feelings—how you are feeling and why you are feeling that way. Try to record significant events of the day and how you felt about each one. Write about the good times, such as a good night's sleep, a weekend away, your first day back to work, or your first outing with a friend. You need to keep in touch with whom you are throughout this traumatic experience—and especially who you are becoming. Keeping in touch with your feelings is very important. It helps you see inside yourself.

When your spouse died, you were surrounded by people—family, friends, neighbors, co-workers, clergy, etc. You were never alone. However, the passage of time sent them all back to their usual routines and you were left with your own life to live—without that one special person who gave meaning and purpose to so much of your day—your spouse. You often wonder how the whole world goes about its business while you're in hell.

You have to reach out. This might be difficult for you, but stoicism will not help. You may never have had to depend on others like you must do now. Never consider yourself a burden. You are not a burden to family and friends. The outpouring of love you receive from them can be a tremendous source of comfort and unity. You wouldn't hesitate to help someone in a time of need, so don't be afraid to ask for something now. People do care, but *you* must take the initiative. Have them run errands for you—the store, the post office, or the bank. They can help you to keep some perspective in your life.

Try to be with those who can accept and understand your emotions. You do not need people around you who feel sorry for you or who continually say, "Don't worry, you will be all right"—especially when you are not all right! Some people will not know what to say to you. They may even avoid you entirely. Do not allow this to hurt you. Expect changes in your relationships. Although your married friends want to include you, their lifestyle is different. You are single now. Your social life may not be couple-oriented anymore, but you can make valuable new friendships with other widowed or single persons.

At this time of change, you would be wise not to make hasty decisions about anything—selling your home, giving away personal belongings of your loved one, making large purchases, or any other major decisions. You will have days when it seems that such a big piece of you has been ripped away and that only a gaping hole is left. You will also have days of celebrating new beginnings in life. Your life will be different now because your roles are different. I experienced many positive changes and I trust that you will too!

When Someone Has Died

O Christ, someone whom I loved very much has died and there is an empty place I cannot fill. My heart aches and inside I feel stiff and tired. Help me, Christ, to look straight at that empty place and not be frightened. Help me to be unafraid to walk the earth without him but to take strength and comfort from your love.

— Avery Brooke, 1975, p. 36

WHEN A PARENT DIES

My Dad

My dad was a very special person to me. He was funny, was very friendly, and everyone loved him. He treated me more as a friend than his daughter, for I was his helper around the house. He loved to imitate Benny Hill's goofy sailor salute and told great dirty jokes. To this day, I do not understand why God took my dad away from me.

It was in May. I was eight years old. It was a week before Mother's Day. My mother gathered me in her arms in the middle of the night. I was unaware of what happened. Later, I woke up in the hospital lobby. It was harshly lit and made everyone a sick color. I remember my grandparents (my dad's parents) were there. I never saw my grandfather look so sad and hopeless. He was usually silly just like his son. I asked my mom what was happening. She said Daddy was sick. When the doctor came in he spoke like a robot. He said words like cat-scan and aneurysm. I didn't know what they meant. For the next few days, I stayed at my mom's friend's house. I read *Madd* magazines all day, not caring what was going on. I still didn't understand what happened. Then one night my mom took me aside and sat me on her knees and looked at me. She looked like she had been crying and was trying hard not to in front of me. She said, "Daddy is dying." I can't remember what she said after that or how I felt. We just hugged and left for the hospital. He was in Intensive Care. It was dark and very dim. My aunts and uncles were gathered around him. He wasn't breathing on his own. He was on a respirator. I cried and cried when I saw him. He already looked dead. I never saw him like that. A couple of days later my mother took him off the respirator because she didn't want him to suffer. My grandmother called her a murderess. That really hurt. My mom gave me the choice of going to the funeral, but I didn't want to. She said he looked very happy and peaceful.

I realize my dad is probably happy and now I'm not afraid of dying. I see him telling dirty jokes to all the angels. I miss him.

Natalie Burns – 11/2/90

Dad

I was usually the caretaker of my father, Ward, in medical matters even though my mother is living. Mom did the at home taking care of him but when it came to dealing with the doctors (particularly on problems and Dad's rights regarding health care) I stepped in. I worked at the Veteran's Administration hospital where my dad was treated until about a year before his death. During that time I always dealt directly with the doctors on his care, was present in the holding room before his surgeries and in the recovery room or the Intensive Care Unit after surgery. I observed in the operating room during one of his minor surgeries. I also was the person who would call the hospital in the middle of the night postoperatively to check on his progress. One time when Mom and Dad were on a trip in Northern California my dad had to have emergency surgery. I spoke with the surgeon by phone before the operation to ease my father's fears. I was the person my father wanted close by when it came to hospitals and doctors.

When my father called to say he was sick late that Thursday night I asked my brother to take him to the hospital. The reason I asked John to take dad was because I was on a new job and was concerned that I might lose my job if I didn't come into work the next day.

When I got to work the next day I called my parent's house. The answer machine answered. About an hour later my brother called to tell me that he heard the message but was on the way to the pharmacy to pick up a prescription for Dad. He said that the hospital said there was nothing wrong with Dad and they gave him a prescription for Vicadan (a strong pain reliever). He said that they had gotten home from the hospital around 3:00 A.M. and that Dad was very tired. John said that Dad told him around 10:00 A.M. that it was okay for John to go to work, so John said he would return around 3:00 P.M. I was not comfortable with there being "nothing wrong" with Dad but I waited until about 12:30 P.M. to call him so that he could get some sleep. No answer. The tape machine came on again. I called John. John said the medicine must have knocked him out and to let him sleep. I called his doctor's office to ask her what was going on. I was promised a call back but one half hour later a clerk from the doctor's office called to say that the doctor was busy seeing patients and she could not call me back. She said I could bring my father into the office. Bring my father into the office? I was thirty miles from his home. I had now tried to call several more times and still no answer. I was on a new job and trying to be very discrete.

I called my brother and told him that I was going to send the paramedics to the house. John was convinced that Dad was sacked out because of the medication. John told me that he would leave work soon and go check on Dad. I got a phone call from my brother about an hour later telling me that Day was okay except that he found him laying on the bathroom floor. Dad had gotten up to go to the bathroom after John went to work and fell on the floor and could not get up.

Over the previous six years the Veterans Administration had replaced and revised my father's left hip joint numerous times. One year before he died (February 1996) he was operated on for what was to be the final hip operation. Four days postop the new joint prothesis was found dislocated. Dad opted to have the surgeons remove the entire prosthesis and that left Dad on crutches. However, Dad should have been able to get up from a fall or at least crawl to the phone.

At any rate, John said that Dad was fine but tired and wanted to be put back in bed. Dad even commented that he probably would not be well enough to go to his AA meeting that evening. I told John that I would be over to relieve him in a couple of hours after I got off work and got a few things done. John called me at 6:45 and said Dad was worse. I told John I was on my way but if he thought the situation was serious to take Dad to the hospital immediately or call the paramedics. John said he would get Dad ready to go to the hospital. I said I would be there in about twenty minutes. I arrived finding five Los Angeles County Sheriff cars, two fire trucks, a paramedic unit, and an ambulance at my parent's house. My brother John said that he was helping Dad dress to go to the hospital when the phone rang. John answered the phone. It was our sister, Jane. Cordless phone in hand, John then turned around and saw that Dad had stopped breathing. The paramedics made a gallant effort to revive him, but as Dad would say, "That is all she wrote." Well, almost "all she wrote."

My parents' neighbor Dick, a retired firefighter, met me out front. Dick asked what I needed. All I could say was "do not leave me." So, joined at the hip, so to speak, Dick guided me into the entry of the house. I was met by a paramedic who told me that my father was not breathing. Dick and I stayed in the entry hall and watched, in horror, as the EMTs who were moving my father to the ambulance, dropped my unconscious father off the side of the backboard onto the garage floor. The EMTs did not strap him down on the backboard and declined the help from the paramedics.

The emergency room physicians' made one more effort to revive Dad before pronouncing him dead. The cause of death is listed as cardiac arrest, probably myocardial infarction (heart attack), but the truth is that we do not really know why he died. We did not ask for an autopsy and I wish we had.

As you can see, it really was a big shock. No one had a clue, particularly not Dad. Dad was not interested in dying. He knew he would not live forever, but he had plans for sticking around for another six or eight years. Dad's death is a great loss and we miss him dearly. We rejoice in knowing that he led a good life and really did live each and every day to its fullest. Dad did not believe in giving up, ever. His hands were knotted by arthritis. That did not stop him from placing his left hand on his right arm to steady it while he signed court cards at his

AA meeting. Dad was unable to walk without the aid of crutches because of the botched hip surgery in January 1996. However, that did not stop him from going to Mexico to fish three times that year, or from attending an AA convention in Honolulu. Unable to golf his last year, Dad still made it to the course twice a week to ride the course with his friend, Frank. Dad enjoyed the benefits of being disabled shopping when at K-Mart he could drive the electric car around the store!

Dad was a practical type guy. He told me once, "When I die, have them burn me up and the next time one of your brothers goes fishing, have him dump me in the ocean." However, Mom said the fishing idea was not okay! He was buried at the National Cemetery in Riverside.

Dad's AA friend, Leroy, asked if he could put a golf club in the casket. We said, "Sure," It was Leroy's best golf club, too. My aunt thought one of the K-Mart coupons for free coffee would be nice. I suggested McDonald's coupons. Then a fishing rod was suggested. Mother said, "That is enough," so we settled for the golf club.

The service was wonderful, warmhearted, and spirited. The chapel was full with love, gentle laughter, and the many people who loved my father.

My father was my hero, but he was not perfect. Through the grace of God he got sober in Alcoholics Anonymous (37 years) and thereafter, he continually tried to be a better person. It is an honor to call Ward my father. I felt very guilty for my father's death because I did not realize the seriousness of his illness and I placed too much importance on the job. My oldest son (age 28) died suddenly and unexpectedly five months and four days after my father. I got fired from the job several months after my son died.

— Kris Cerone

> I was astonished to hear a highly intelligent boy of ten remark after the sudden death of his father: "I know father's dead, but what I can't understand is why he doesn't come home to supper."
> — Sigmund Freud, 1996, p. 377
> excerpt from *The Last Dance*

Daddy

It is thirty-three years, almost to the day, the man in my life went to work and never came back. He was forty-three and my father. I was Daddy's little girl.

When anyone will listen, I speak of him. I was in love with him and him with me. He took me everywhere, made me laugh, tucked me in. I still see him every time I see my brother's hands and my sister's green eyes. I, however, look like my mother.

My son has his sense of humor and easy ways. I'm often saddened to think they've never met. I tell my son about him and sometimes wonder if I should. Am I expecting him to live up to some fantasy? Why can't I let this go?

Fathers are not something to let go. They teach and guide and shape your life. I remember the times we shared star gazing, the Christmas Eve he woke me up to see the new fallen snow and the canoe at a lake. To remember makes me sad. I can still grieve for the loss of these seemingly unimportant events.

The grieving comes further and further apart as time goes by. But I'm always thankful for it. Without it, he'd be gone.

— Anonymous Student

Walter, My Dad

I can still remember the phone call like it happened yesterday. It was 5:00 A.M. and the when the phone rang, it startled me out of sleep. My mom's voice was so shaky, I hardly recognized it. She said, "I'm at Long Island Jewish Hospital with Dad. He's had a heart attack and it's very touch and go." I was barely able to say what came out next, which was "Okay, I'm on my way, Mom. Take it easy. I love you." I hung up and all I remember is my mind racing. I was trying to get dressed and couldn't even remember which came first, the sweater or the bra! My husband just looked at me with such an expression of what should I do? He tried to reassure me my dad would be okay. I raced to get dressed and yelled at my husband to stay home with our children. I didn't want them to wake up to a neighbor at our house. At the same time, I said "Oh, my God, I have to call my brother and sister." I called my sister first. She lived in Manhattan and I knew she could get to Mom first. Then, I called my brother's house. He lived upstate, New York. I spoke to my sister-in-law whom all I really remember her saying was, "Don't drive by yourself." I hung up feeling really cold, scared and out of my mind. I remember in the midst of getting dressed, looking at my husband and saying, "Oh, My God! What if he doesn't make it?!" We hugged and I ran out of the house. I guess to try and describe the drive from Sayville, Long Island to Queens was like long, dark, and cold—like being on auto pilot. I remember speeding and thinking in my mind that if only a cop would stop me and I could tell him the story that he would give me a police escort which would get me there faster. The ride was long and lonely to say the least. I couldn't remember the exit for the hospital although I had been there numerous times in the past for other reasons and had also lived not two miles from the hospital all my life. I stopped at a gas station just barely. I actually drove through, rolled the window down and yelled "Where's the hospital?" The attendant directed me as I pulled out the other side of the station. My only other memory of the car ride was of pounding my fists on the steering wheel and yelling for my dad to hold on because I was on my way. I don't remember parking the car, and to this day, I could not tell you where I parked it—somewhere near the emergency room entrance. I guess the only way to explain the next few moments would be sheer terror and a feeling of emptiness. I walked through the door, gave the receptionist my name and as soon as I did, she stood up and came around the corner to walk me into my mother. It was at that moment that I knew he was dead. The lady's facial expression and body language said it all. I was brought to where my mom and sister were and we just hugged and cried. We were the three closest women in his life. I remember feeling scared for my mom. Would she make it through this? She looked so shocked and frail. It seemed like a movie about someone else's life. My sister looked lost. I asked to see my dad. I didn't know why then, but I have since learned that I needed closure and to be sure he was dead. After all, this was so sudden! It all seemed so strange that just forty-eight hours before this we had all been together with him—including my brother from upstate. We were all together for my dad's best friend's funeral. This was incomprehensible to me. My last memory of my dad was his arm around me out at the grave side. It really made me wonder about spirituality and God when I thought to myself—what were the chances that we would all come together in October of 1989? We weren't supposed to do that until Thanksgiving!

— Linda Ciavarelli

*   *   *

Of all the deaths that may be experienced in childhood, the most affecting is considered to be the death of a parent. A parent's death is perceived as a loss of security, nurturing, and affection—a loss of the emotional and psychological support upon which the child relied prior to the death. Many people assume that children are not capable of experiencing true grief; as a result, their reactions to death are not often fully explored and evaluated. Children certainly do grieve, but their ways of expressing it are different from those of adults. Differences in mourning are determined by both the cognitive and emotional development of a child. It is important to recognize that the work of mourning may not end in quite the same way for a child as it does for an adult. Mourning for a childhood loss can be revived at many points in an adult's life when it is triggered during important life events, such as a graduation or a wedding. One of the most obvious examples is when the child reaches the same age as the parent who died. When this mourning is reactivated, it does not necessarily indicate pathology but is simply a further illustration of "working through."

Children feel the same range of emotions as adults, but these feelings may not be obvious to the observer. They can be laughing and playing normally one minute, and crying and needing comfort the next. Adults may misinterpret this shift in attention and the accompanying emotions as an incapacity to feel the loss deeply. It is typical for children to establish a set of memories, feelings, and actions that serve to aid them in reconstructing an image of the dead parent. This helps the child remain in a relationship with the deceased. As the child matures and the grief lessens, the child reexamines the meaning of the loss over time. Although the loss is permanent and unchanging, the process of coping with it is not.

Like the young child, adolescents also respond in a unique way to the death of a parent. Adolescents may show intense emotional reactions, including confusion, depression, guilt, and anger. These symptoms may continue over a long period of time. When this occurs in childhood or adolescence, the child may fail to adequately mourn and later in life may often present with symptoms of depression or the inability to form close relationships during adult years.

In addition, physical complaints and difficulties with eating and sleeping are also common. Many adolescents attempt to hide their inner feelings of hurt and pain in an effort to appear "grown-up." As a result, they may refuse to allow themselves the support of others because they want to demonstrate their control or because of fear they will be perceived as abnormal or different. What others think, especially peers, is extremely important at this age.

A parent's sudden death often leaves adult children with a sense of abandonment and even panic that catches us by surprise. We may have lived enough years to be an adult but we will always be a child in relation to our parents. Even if we are "parenting our parents" before their deaths, it is the parent of our childhood that we bury. The world appears to be a different place after our parents die.

The death of a parent represents the loss of a long-term relationship characterized by love, nurture, and unconditional support. A parent's death is an important symbolic event for middle-age adults. Many have reported their outlook on life changes. They begin to examine their lives more closely, to begin changing what they don't like, and to appreciate more fully their ongoing relationships.

As adults, we are seldom ready for a parent's death. We may be busy raising our families or engrossed in our careers. We may be spending much of our free time traveling or striving to settle down. We may be living close or far away from where our parents live. Whatever the circumstances, it is almost impossible to prepare ourselves emotionally for the death of a parent. It is unfortunate that people attempt to console us by saying, "Your father lived a long and successful life" or "You should be happy you had so many good years with your mother." These phrases are painful to hear when our wonderful father or loving mother is lying in a casket. The sorrow is still very deep and very real.

The death of a parent is the most common form of bereavement in our country. However, the unspoken message is that when a parent is elderly, the death is somehow considered less a loss than other deaths.

Find ways to cry and talk. Share your grief as long as you feel the need. More than likely, many family members will be satisfied hearing you talk about your deceased parent. Many times, friends, especially those who have not experienced the death of a parent, may be more inclined to ask how your day is doing since your mother's death than about how you are coping. Try not to let this upset you. Use it as an opening to express your own feelings.

If you need to talk to your parent, do it! When you look in the mirror and see a resemblance to your mother, tell her. When you say something that reminds you of your dad, let him know. Just saying "Mom" or "Dad" aloud—or whatever name you used—can be a comfort to you.

> Let tears flow of their own accord: their flowing is not inconsistent with peace and harmony.
> — Seneca, stoic philosopher (4 B.C.-65 A.D.)

WHEN A CHILD DIES

AnnMarie

My daughter, AnnMarie, died on November 12, 1990, at approximately nine o'clock in the morning, as a result of a traffic accident while returning home from a college seminar. Her passing has forever changed the lives of everyone who knew her. We all look at things differently now. A beautiful sunset, an autumn day, wild flowers in a field, objects of beauty, all the things that we take for granted in our daily lives are things that she will never see again. Her memory will always be a part of us all.

In 1964, I married Orlando, and soon after, we started our family. We had four children who were born into a loving family and community of friends. All the years that our children were growing up were filled with the normal ups and downs that most families experience.

Our children, Carmen, Christine, AnnMarie, and Angela all had wonderful friends throughout their growing years who impacted their lives and grew with them into wonderful, mature, and loving human beings.

On November 12, 1990, at 3:00 A.M., Orlando and I received the phone call that no parent ever wants to get. We were told that AnnMarie was injured in an automobile accident in Scranton, Pennsylvania, and was in very serious condition. We arrived at the hospital four hours later. We were able to be with AnnMarie for another two hours before she passed away. During these hours, two of our dear friends left Waterbury to meet us at the hospital and to later drive us home. We were given her personal effects that day by a hospital social worker. When we arrived home, I put her clothes in her room.

During the two weeks that followed AnnMarie's funeral, our home was filled with many friends and family members who helped write out thank you responses for all the donations of food, flowers, memorials, and mass cards received during this time of our grief. By the time two weeks had passed, we had written out 850 thank-you cards.

The solace that I find when I start to feel the impact of her loss is the belief that if she were able to have such an effect on all here on GOD'S earth, then imagine the effect she has on everyone up in Heaven.

AnnMarie belonged to all of us. She is our daughter, sister, relative, and friend. We will keep her in our hearts until the day when we will all be together again.

— Iris Romeo

Bobby

It was a beautiful sunny February day, the 17th to be exact. We had recently had a new snowfall so the ground was covered with a beautiful covering of white. The schools were closed due to President's Day so the kids were home making plans on how to take advantage of the day. Bobby, who was seventeen and a senior in high school was finishing up his term paper for graduation. He was so excited that day, the sun and snow seemed to put him in a jubilant mood. He was working very hard on his paper and laughing and jumping around the house all at the same time. After he finished his paper he called a few of his great friends and they made plans to go to a trailer they have in the woods. They spend a lot of time there, just working outside in the woods and spending precious time together. He came down the steps and asked me if he could pick up his friend Erin and then go and get the rest of the gang, which on that day would consist of Chad, Eric, and Amy. He said that they wanted to do some target shooting along with doing some odds and ends around the trailer. I told him sure, just so he was back before 4:30. He got so excited to be able to go out into the woods. Sometimes I think the woods was Bobby's first home, and ours his second. Adding to his excitement was being with his friends. Bobby and his group were exceptionally close. They spent so much time together, never arguing, just as Bobby would say "hanging together" . . . so Bobby gathered up his gear to go out into the woods. He dressed in his favorite "outdoor" clothes, my green sweater, a pair of cords, his dad's coat, his awesome doc martens, and to complete the outfit his favorite blue hat! He got into the gun cabinet and got out the guns. His dad's 22 pistol and his own rifle. I've seen him do this many times as Bobby was an avid hunter. I reminded him to be home by 4:30 and he looked at me and said, "I'll be home way before then". . . and he laughed and out the door he went. When the kids arrived at the lane that led up to the trailer, Bobby and his friend Chad started to shoot before they entered the woods. Bobby took some shots with the pistol and then handed the gun to Chad. Bobby then ran up through the woods and grabbed a hold of Erin and was joking around with her. Chad was going to shoot and then didn't which advanced the gun in the chamber. Later in the day when they got to the tailor Bobby took some shots with the rifle, and then took a hold of the pistol. He shot at a few things and then the gun clicked empty. For some unknown reason, Bobby raised the gun to his head and it clicked again, and then again, but the third time he did it the advanced bullet came out and he was shot through the head. I was at home typing on the computer when the phone rang. I will never forget the ring of that phone. The voice on the other end said to me "Becky, you have to get out to the trailer. There has been an accident and Bobby shot himself." I don't remember much except that I knew I had to call Bobby's dad and tell him to get to the trailer because Bobby had my car and I had no way. I told him to go straight there and I would find a way. I ran to my friend's house and they took me out to the road that leads to the trailer. The trailer sets up in the woods a good distance. I don't really know how far, but on that day it seemed to stretch for miles. When I arrived at the road leading to the trailer, Amy and Erin were there. When they saw me, they began to cry and I knew that it wasn't good. I started up into the woods and police officers stopped me and told me that the paramedics were up there and that I wasn't to go up. I tried to get past them but they wouldn't let me go. So I stood with my husband and we waited for them to bring my son to me. The snow in the woods was much deeper than the snow was in town, so it took them a while to get down through the woods. One of Bobby's friends worked for the ambulance crew and when I saw him carrying Bobby through the woods he was crying and collapsed. I ran up to the stretcher when they were coming down through the woods and there beside Bobby were his friends Chad and Eric. Eric was talking to Bobby as if he were walking right beside him. I looked at Bobby, who was still breathing and told him to be good, and to listen. I grabbed Eric and Chad and we exited the woods. They loaded Bobby into the ambulance and took him to our local hospital, where everyone that had now heard the news gathered. Bobby was a very popular boy in town because he wasn't judgmental, he talked to anyone and everyone, and never had anything bad to say about another person. They decided they needed to life flight him to a trauma hospital . . . so that was arranged. Bob and I loaded the car with some things we needed and our other son, Dylan. So we set off hoping and praying that we would receivce some good news. One of the hardest things to do was to leave our youngest son, Caleb, with friends not telling him what happened. When we arrived at the trauma center they told us that Bobby was in a room, our hearts fell. Because they didn't have Bobby in surgery, we knew that the outlook was not good. At 10:00 P.M. that evening they told us that Bobby was brain dead. They asked us if we wanted to take the kids in to see him, which at this time were many. They had made the one hour long trip to sit and wait and pray with us. We took them in a few at a time, and watched as they said "see ya later" to their friend. The second thing in my life harder to watch than my son dying was watching those young innocent children saying goodbye so soon in life to a friend. Bobby was an organ donor, so the process after that was long and tiring. At 3:00 A.M., we left the trauma hospital for home without our oldest son. It was the worse ride of my life. The days to follow are just a blur. The viewing and the funeral . . . and the days that follow have just seemed to run together. I have found that I do my son a great injustice to focus on the date of February 17th when he had seventeen wonderful years to look at. I read somewhere that it's not the dates in 1979-1997 that matters . . . it's the dash in between because that represents his life. And what a good life he had. I found later that when Bobby was shot, Amy ran ahead to call the ambulance at a house down the lane. And then Erin, Chad, and Eric started to carry him out of the woods. I find comfort in knowing this, and believe that Bobby didn't die in a hospital in Johnstown, Pennsylvania . . . he died when his friends that he loved set him down in the woods that were his home, and he let go of their hands and reached and grabbed the hands of God. Amy's death was a year from the date of Bobby's funeral. Actually, that is why they were all out there together. They took a ride on Bobby's favorite road in remembrance of him. They wrecked and Amy was killed. And so it will be, that he will pass from this world being with his friends and doing the activity that he most enjoyed in life. It's ironic when I think of it, all that he enjoyed also became that which stole his life from him. The story can go on and on. Bobby is cremated and his urn sits here at our home, but at a cemetery not far from home sits a tombstone that reads "Amy and Bobby, together forever floating with the moon and the stars". . . and I believe that together they are . . . and someday I, too, will be with them.

— Becky Gwinn

Chris

Chris was born in June of 1980, on Jim's birthday, as a matter of fact, Flag Day! Ryan was eighteen months old when Chris arrived. I almost lost Chris twice while pregnant with him. At ten weeks I began bleeding, that lasted for three weeks. That resolved, then I had an appendectomy while pregnant with him! So when he was born healthy, I was elated. I had been concerned with all that had happened while pregnant with him, but he was perfect. When Chris was eighteen months old, we had another close call. We were visiting down in Texas, on our trip home, we drove about two hours into the thirty-hour drive when Chris got sick. He stayed that way for the whole trip home— vomiting, diarrhea, high temperature, the works. When we got home, I took him to the doctor. He was very sick! He was immediately admitted to the hospital . . . he had Salmonella, came so close to dying—he was so dehydrated. He spent ten days in the hospital. After that it was smooth sailing for Chris. Chris excelled at everything he pursued. He was very sociable, and so damn cute, loved by all. He was a great student and a wonderful athlete, a really complete individual. He was the starting pitcher for his little league team, and played short stop as well! Not bad for a lefty, huh? They won the championship, with Chris at the plate. He was also a star soccer player. The only child from our town in his age group to make the premier district team. He was a striker, a natural scorer, and a real finesse player. A joy to watch, a true joy! I used to go and watch all of Chris's practices. I couldn't get enough of watching him play. About a month before Chris died, I sat at a practice, taking in his skillful play and thought, "This is what life's all about." And on the way home, I told him how happy he made me. About two weeks before his death I had a conversation with him. I asked if he felt as if he was missing out on too much because of his commitment to soccer. He often had to miss dances or birthday parties because of soccer. He was playing on two teams at the time, and on his off days he assisted me in coaching Kyle's soccer team, so it was soccer seven days a week for him! He told me that he was happiest on the soccer field, and that he was doing what made him happy. I'm so glad now that I had that conversation with him.

On the day of Chris's accident, I had made a trip to New York City. My brother Mark was in the city for a buyer's convention. Mark was living in San Antonio at the time. He was a toys and health and beauty aids buyer for K-Mart or somewhere like that. My brother Dan was stationed at West Point at the time, and Dan's in-laws live here locally. So Dan's family was visiting with his in-laws for the weekend. Mark came here the night before and in the morning Dan met us here and we all took a train into New York. The convention was a big bore. Dan and I were eager to be done with it! Of course, we probably shared that with Mark as well. So Dan and I finally bid our adieus to Mark. As we headed for the train station, we decided to stop and get something to eat—oh, how I wish we had just gone straight to the train station. That hour may have saved Chris's life! It was weird, the whole way home I talked to Dan about Chris, not the other boys, just focused on Chris. Which was unusual, as I usually bored my captive audiences with news of all my boys! Dan's car was at the train station, so Dan was just going to drop me and run. His wife had expected him earlier than we were actually returning home. Well, when we pulled up in front of my home, there were about three police cars in the area, none of them actually in front of my home. But it was rather curious. As I was getting out of the car, thankfully Dan had not pulled away yet, I noticed through my window, there were some police officers in my home. I suddenly felt TERROR! I asked Dan to come in with me. As I entered my home, the police stopped me, asked if I had a twelve-year-old son, which I replied yes to, Ryan was twelve, Chris was only eleven. They said that there had been an accident. I asked how bad it was and they said they didn't know, that my son had been taken to Yale New Haven Hospital. We were having our house remodeled, almost gutting the house, a $90,000 job! The contractor had, the week before, placed about fifteen sheets of extra long sheetrock leaning against the hall wall, he had it all clamped together for safety reasons. The sheetrock had somehow fallen to the other side of the hall, and pinned Chris at the throat. Jim had left Chris home reading a book for school, while he went to drop off an article he had written about Chris's team. He was gone with Kyle for about forty minutes, when he returned home, he found Chris pinned by the sheetrock, pulse-less and without respirations. My poor seven-year-old

Kyle made this discovery with him. As I rounded the corner, I saw police tape going across the hall. I went to the area, but was told by the officers that I couldn't go near there. They told me that my other children were down the street at a neighbor's house, and that Jim had gone to the hospital with my son. Now mind you, I am thinking that this is Ryan who was injured. He was a bit of a klutz and accident prone, so it all seemed to fit! Well, the police were giving us directions to the hospital when the phone rang. It was Jim! He told me that he had no pulse, that he had to do CPR. I was losing it quick, and the weird thing was that Jim never mentioned Chris's name either. He said that they were working on him in the ER, and that he didn't know much about what was happening. I hung up from Jim, continued to get directions from the police to the hospital. And just then Ryan arrived! I saw him and almost passed out. I had a moment of elation. I thought, you stupid people. It wasn't my son, and here he is safe! Well, the elation lasted for just a moment when I realized that, "Oh, my God, it's Chris." Chris always seemed more fragile to me. I know it's silly but when I thought it was Ryan, I had thought, Ryan is a tough guy—he can handle anything! But Chris was a different story. The police had asked me to stop down at the neighbor's house to see Kyle on my way to the hospital, as he had been through a lot, with the ambulance and all. Ryan seemed to be in shock, unable to speak. So off I went to the neighbors with Ryan to see Kyle. Thank goodness Dan was still there. I don't know how I would have gotten to the hospital myself. Kyle was also in terrible shape. He just kept saying, "I don't want my Chris to die." I couldn't hear that. I just had to go to make my Chris better. As we traveled to the hospital, I knew in my heart that Chris had little hope of survival. I kept hearing Jim's words to me . . . "I had to do CPR on him." Being a medical professional, I realize that when a heart stops, the chances of the person surviving that insult to the brain is slim. As I entered the emergency room I immediately saw a Milford police officer. I knew that he must be here because of Chris. I identified myself and asked how Chris was. He was very uneasy with me and said he didn't know his condition. He asked me to follow him. I can't describe the overwhelming feeling of dread as he led me to a room that I know well, a room that is known in the hospital as the "bereavement room." I knew just what being in this room meant. As I entered, I was hit by even more assurance that this was serious, as I found a priest present in this small room with my husband. To make a long story short, Chris did not survive the accident. He lived for thirty hours. The nurses removed Chris from the ventilator and pulled the tube that he had going into his lungs. At our request they quickly placed Chris in our arms. He laid across Jim's and my lap as if he was sleeping. For a brief moment I prayed that he would take a breath, although I knew that was not possible. His brain was dead and he would never take a breath again. I resolved myself to allowing Chris to die. I have never been able to explain to anyone what I felt at the moment of his death. It was a profoundly peaceful moment as he passed from one existence to another. I was overcome by a feeling of peacefulness. It was a feeling I have never had before and think I will never have again. It is not really possible to put it into words. Jim and I sat for a moment holding Chris in our arms. We kissed him and expressed our love for him. I am not sure how long passed until we placed his body back into the bed. We left the ICU and told all our friends and family that Chris had died. There were many tears and hugs. This horrible ordeal had come to an end, or so I thought. I could not have known what was ahead of us for years to follow. Our new life had just begun. Our life without Chris.

— Beth McCarthy

Casey

Casey was born a few minutes after midnight on Friday 13, 1984. The nurse thought we would be upset by the fact it was Friday the 13th but Casey's mom was born on a Friday the 13th, so we thought it was a great thing. He was our third child and we were thrilled to have him. It took us five long years to have a child and we were so happy to now have our third healthy and beautiful child. Casey grew up in a good neighborhood where the children played up and down the streets. He was a happy child and most loving. Teachers would tell about his constant hugs and his wonderful smile. One of the things Casey loved to do was go with his dad and brother hunting. On Father's Day, 1994, he had his good friend and former neighbor, Adam, spend the night with him. Adam was eleven and he and Casey both played baseball at our little league park. On Monday, they got up and watched some television, but it was a beautiful day and they got restless. Casey asked his mother if they could go over to the school and play on the newly renovated playground. The boys went to the playground but somehow decided to explore and ended up on a railroad trestle over a creek. As they looked down over the creek, a freight train with eighty-two cars came around the curve. The boys had no escape route and were trapped. We had a double funeral with a tremendous turnout and quite a tribute to two fine young men that were well-liked in the community. They are laid to rest in adjoining plots and are forever in our hearts.

— Frank and Beth

Anthony

On October 29, 1995, I gave birth to my first child. A beautiful, healthy little guy that I named Anthony Michael. As months passed, I watched in great delight as Anthony learned and explored his new world. He was the sunshine in my life. He supplied me with more smiles and laughs than one could imagine.

On June 30, 1996, my nightmare began. We awoke to find Anthony laying lifeless in his crib. He was a victim to Sudden Infant Death Syndrome. My beautiful eight-month-old little boy was gone from my arms forever. We tried CPR and he was rushed by a fire ambulance to a local hospital where they tried to revive him for forty-five minutes with no luck. I knew what the doctor was going to say as soon as he walked into the room. Those words still ring through my head today. "I'm sorry, there was nothing we could do for him." I think a part of me died with him.

We held the wake and funeral at a local home and he was buried in Babyland at a cemetery on July 3, 1996. I had many feelings, at first I wanted to believe that perhaps it was a bad dream—that maybe I could just wake up and all would be fine. Then came the blame game. I blamed everyone I could think of—even God. Then the anger set in. I was so mad. My little boy was gone and I was left childless, wondering if I was still a mommy. I found out that I am still a mommy. I will always have my son that died. He lives in my heart every day. I then went through the sadness—intense sadness. It came about five or six months after he died. I have heard people say that is when the numbness wears off. I did not want to even get out of bed, but I knew I had to. It was right about that time I found out I was pregnant again.

Now, two years later, I can say that Anthony made me a better person. I graduated from high school through adult education with a 4.0 grade point average. He gives me strength in my life. I know that I have a special little angel watching over my family now. After two years I can also say that it is easier. I am no longer angry or blame people. I have accepted that he is gone. Don't get me wrong. I would give anything to change it, but I know that I can't. I still have my days—some worse than others. The anniversary dates are the hardest. I know that he is with me though. I love and miss my son greatly. I have learned many lessons from his death. I am now a parent contact and an online counselor for a loss of a child website. I wish that there was no need to write this story, that none of us ever have to go through the pain of losing a child, but on the other hand I hope that you have found some comfort in knowing that you are not alone in this journey we call grief.

— Traci Clayton

Shelley Maria

My twenty-year-old daughter Shelley Maria was murdered November 29, 1993. Shelley was spending the night with a friend, Lynnette. Lynnette was being stalked by a former boyfriend, Mark. Around 6:00 A.M. Mark broke into the apartment in a drunken and drug induced rage and murdered both girls with a sawed off shotgun. Lynnette shot Mark once and was able to hit him in the arm before he murdered her. Mark left the apartment bleeding and went to his home and called his brother for help. Mark was taken to the hospital emergency room and there the brother told the nurse somebody should go and check on the apartment because Mark had told him that Lynnette had shot him. Police did not arrive at the apartment until after 7:00 A.M. Around 8:15 A.M. Shelley's office called and told me she had not arrived at work and wondered if I knew if she had car trouble or something. I told them she would have called me if that were the case and I had not heard from her. I left my office and drove to the apartment after I did not get an answer on the phone.

Lynnette had gotten in the habit of getting up all night to look out and check her car because two weeks prior Mark had vandalized it. I thought maybe they had overslept. I remember coming to the intersection just a block away from the apartment and seeing police cars everywhere. When I drove up a man was standing in the street and I read his lips, "Now who the hell is this?" I remember jumping out of my car and going straight toward him. He asked who I was and what I was doing there. I told him my name and that it was my daughter's car (pointing toward an automobile) and I wanted to see her. He looked at me and then told me my daughter had been murdered. All I remember then was that there was this sensation of something, life, draining out of me. I had spoken with her the night before around 10:00 P.M. and asked the girls not to stay at Lynnette's apartment. I wanted them to come out to our house in the country. Shelley's last words to me were "Now Mama, don't start that. We are okay. The police are watching the apartment. I love you, Mama. I'll talk to you tomorrow." Mark was arrested that day in the hospital. After surgery he was later transferred to the county jail. On December 19, 1993, Mark was found dead in his cell from suicide.

It has been five years this November. I am a totally different person. My reasoning and ideals have changed drastically. I never knew what hate really meant until November 29, 1993. I started attending a support group, Parents of Murdered Children and Other Survivors of Homicide Victims, the next year. Had it not been for the strength of the members in that group I would not have been able to go on. Through the others I have gained strength to carry on.

When Mark committed suicide, the case ended. There could be no trial. My husband and I have had to wrestle with this because we will never be able to see that he is punished. Nowhere is it legally written that Mark murdered my Shelley. Years from now someone may see Shelley's tombstone and wonder what happened to such a young person.

— Alice F. Burton

Sydnie Claire

Saturday, June 14, 1997. We did our normal Saturday things. Later in the afternoon, on impulse, I wanted to see how my best friend Belinda's house was coming along. She and her husband, Mike, were building a house and I hadn't been there in some time to see the progress. Martin and Sydnie were thrilled to go. I figured Mike would be out there as usual on Saturday afternoon. Well, neither of them were there when we got there—so we rode on down to a little store and I bought each of the kids a bag of chips and a cola. I remember them both telling me they loved me when I got back to the car with their treats.

We passed one more time in front of Belinda and Mike's to see if they were there, but they weren't. I pulled up to the stop sign on the highway and thought maybe we could go visit another friend, Janna, whom I hadn't seen in a couple months. Martin and Sydnie enjoyed playing with Janna's two boys just a few months earlier at Mardi Gras. Janna is a friend from high school. We walked in each other's weddings. We didn't see each other much, but when we did talk, we always picked up where we left off. So I called Janna from the cell phone and asked her if it would be okay to come visit. She said, "Sure." Martin and Sydnie were thrilled. I called my husband Steven, to let him know where we would be. He asked me "What are you going there for?" and I said "Just to visit." God, had I known . . .

It was about 5:30 P.M. when we got there. Janna had some friends over and there were several other kids there in addition to her boys. The grown-ups were visiting in the kitchen and the kids were going in and out from room to room and playing outside in the front yard having a good time. I did as I always do and got up every few minutes to go see what the kids were doing. I always like to know what they're doing and make sure they are not getting into something they aren't supposed to. I had friends tell me on several occasions, "Ju, don't worry about them, they're fine." Or "Ju, you worry so much, they're just playing." I've been teased that if I watched them any closer they'd be attached by a string. But I always had to know what they were doing.

Sydnie came to sit on my lap and put her arms around my neck. She had a ring of chocolate icing around her mouth from the cupcake she had just eaten. She told me "Mommy, I love you." I smiled, hugged her and said "I love you, too, Syd." Just a few minutes later I went to check on the kids, yet again. They were all in the front yard playing, except Sydnie. My heart went to my toes at that moment. I just knew where I'd find my baby. I ran through the house, out the back door, flew up the steps to the pool and found my precious little girl floating face down in the pool. I screamed like I had never ever screamed in my life. And I was frozen where I stood. One of Janna's friends was right behind me and pulled Sydnie out of the pool. I couldn't stop screaming. I was screaming and jumping up and down and screaming. I couldn't believe what I had seen. NOOOOOO, NOOOO, SYDNIE NO, MY BABY, SYDNIE NOOOOO . . . This just was NOT true, it was NOT happening. Someone called 911. I started screaming at Sydnie, BREATHE, BABY, BREATHE FOR MOMMY. PLEEAASSEEEE, SYDNIE, BREATHE . . . I called Steven, my mom, and left a message on Belinda's machine to meet us at the hospital from my cell phone, while Janna's husband, Reggie, and a family friend of their's did CPR on my baby.

The ambulance got there, the sheriff and sherrif's deputies. They put me in a sheriff's deputy car to take me to the hospital. I wanted to ride in the ambulance. They wouldn't let me. I didn't want to leave my baby!!!!! Finally, the ambulance caught up with us and we escorted it to the hospital.

We get to the hospital. Steven finally got there and I just knew he'd never ever speak to me because I had let this happen. Sydnie was with me and I was supposed to be protecting her and watching over her. He held me in his arms as best he could. He was shaking. Our hearts were beating very rapidly. We were both so scared. Family and friends started showing up at the hospital.

I felt like I was just going to throw up. I was so nauseated and so petrified. I have never felt anything like that in my entire life. I kept begging Daddy (my deceased father), "Please, Daddy, please, make her better. Talk to God, ask Him to make her okay. Daddy . . . pleaseeeeee, you HAVE to help her. Make her heart start beating again, Daddy." And then I started praying like I never have.

I am thankful that our closest family and friends were there when we got the news shortly after 8:24 P.M. that Sydnie didn't make it. My baby was gone. I remember throwing myself at Steven and pounding on his chest screaming NO, NO, NO, NO. All I could do was wail. I couldn't cry anymore. The hairs on my neck still stand up and chills run down my spine when I think about that moment! The emergency room doctor and nurses were wrong. Sydnie was going to be fine. They all just stood there watching me and Steven. I remember screaming at them to get the*&^%$# (very bad word) out, stop *&^%$# (very bad word, again) staring at us. LEAVE US ALONE. I was shocked that those words came tumbling out of my mouth. But this was the most horrifying moment in a parent's life. We didn't need an audience of strangers.

We went into the emergency room when they had her cleaned up. They never did get a heartbeat. I'm told that drowning happens very fast and is one of the least painful deaths. I sure hope they're right. I can't bear the thought that my baby suffered! She was so beautiful, peaceful lying there. My beautiful little girl. I just sat and rocked her and held her and stroked her cheeks. She didn't smell like my Sydnie Claire though. She smelled like chlorine and vomit from the CPR. I wanted to smell her again. I wanted to memorize her scent. She started to get cold and all I wanted to do was warm her up—bring her back. I held her and loved her for as long as I could. I expected her to wake up any minute and say "Hi, Mommy." It looked as though she was just sleeping. She started to get heavy and Steven took her from me so he could say goodbye, too. We had a priest come to give her the last rites. And I sang "You Are My Sunshine" to her one last time. And then I had to leave my baby there.

The thought of how I was going to tell Martin was almost more than I could bear. How could I tell my son that his little sister had died and was never ever coming home again. I just had to tell him fourteen months earlier that his Paw Paw (grandfather) died. They were best friends. Sure, they fought like cats and dogs, but they really loved each other and enjoyed playing together. I don't know how they did it, but Adrienne and Marion, my sisters, are the ones who went to pick up Martin from Janna's house and the ones who told him that Sydnie didn't make it. I thank God for giving them the strength to do that for Steven and me.

The day after Sydnie Claire died, I remember going to the cemetery to see Daddy. I was so angry at him at first for not making Sydnie better. He always made everything better. Anything that would go wrong. Daddy would fix it. I was his little girl, and I wanted him to make MY little girl all better! I realized how irrational I was being. Under the circumstances I think I was entitled. But I talked to Daddy and told him how sorry I was for being mad at him and to watch over Sydnie Claire for me until I would be with them again one day. She was with her Paw. And if she couldn't be with me, who better than to be with her Paw Paw.

We buried her three days later on June 17, 1997. The weather that day was horrible. It rained and flooded most of the day. I remember the moments prior to us viewing Sydnie for the first time. I was sooo scared. I didn't know if she'd look like my Sydnie Claire or not. I need not have worried. She was absolutely GORGEOUS. Her makeup and hair were perfect. She was truly an angel. I told Kenny, the guy at the funeral home who prepared her, what a wonderful job he did—how beautiful she was. He told me that it was nothing that he did—Sydnie was just a beautiful little girl.

People must have thought I was nuts when they came to pay their last respects. I was grabbing everyone by the hand leading them to Sydnie. I wanted to show them my baby, how very beautiful my ANGEL was. We didn't realize it that night just how many people came to offer their condolences. Later, we counted over 1,000 people who signed the guest book.

A family friend of Daddy's came up to me as I was at Sydnie's side (which I hardly left) holding her hand and asked me if I ever touched an angel before. I said no, and he said you are right now. I cried, again. I was in such a state of numbness, shock, disbelief. I still am at times. When we were getting ready to leave the funeral home for the church, I hugged my little girl one last time and asked her to send Mommy and Daddy a rainbow.

That evening Steven was at his mom's. I had gone to my mom's. I get a call from him. "Ju, she sent us a rainbow. There's a rainbow. Go outside and see the rainbow." He hung up. I ran outside. I missed the rainbow, but saw the most beautiful pink sunset I had ever seen in my entire life. A co-worker of mine sent me an e-mail the next day and asked if I had seen the rainbow. He said it was a faint, small rainbow. He said that Sydnie just needs practice before she can make a bigger one!

I'll never ever forget June 14, 1997. I am still haunted by the image of finding Sydnie in that pool. I belong to The Compassionate Friends, which is a support group for bereaved parents. Martin and I go to the Grief Center, which is a local support group for siblings who have lost siblings and their parents. I am also seeing a priest to help me deal with the trauma of Sydnie's death. Without these resources and the help of God, I don't think I would still be here today.

I miss my little girl more than any words can ever express. The physical and mental pain is just beyond comprehension. I'll never understand how I managed to make it this long without my little girl. There is only one explanation I can come up with. By the Grace of God, I go on. But I'll never, ever forget. Sydnie Claire—I'll love her forever. My baby she'll always be!

— Julie "Ju" Smith

JustJu@AOL.com
http://www.geocities.com/Heartland/acres/6627/

My Understanding

My Children are the Greatest Gift God has ever given me
throughout my life experiences. My Children have enriched my life,
and I thank God every day for this Special Blessing.
I always knew that you were only borrowed.
And, one day, you would be the one
I would have to return Home too soon.
This has been my biggest cross, as your Mother
to carry on my journey back Home.
Now, I understand some of the pain Mary felt,
as her Son died on the Cross. And, my total Devotion
of the Consecration to Jesus Christ, the Incarnate Wisdom
through the Blessed Virgin Mary.
When God called you Home, the Angels came to take you by the Hand,
leading you along the shining path
of the place of Peace and light.
You are Home at last,
as you saw the Lord open His arms,
welcoming you with a smile into the everlasting Joy,
that is His Love.
This has been a very heavy cross to everyone you left behind.
But, I know you will be like an angel for each one of us,
until we too are called Home to the Lord.

I will see you later in Heaven
with Faith, Hope and Charity,
while my love, hugs, precious memories
and selfishness remains here in the earthly world
With the Grace of God, until I am with you again.

Love Mom
I love you very much and I will see you later.

Please pray for all family members and friends
who are holding any negative emotions,
such as guilt, anger, and resentment. And for the Peace of Christ.

In Loving Memory of Rebecca Lynn Gwizdala
Mass on October 5, 1996
— Copyright © 1996
Pamela M. Graul-Gwizdala

*   *   *

A difficult loss, which impinges heavily on family equilibrium, is the
death of a child. The death of a child evokes the highest intensities of

bereavement and the widest range of reactions. A study by Sanders (1979) showed death anxiety to be higher for parents, with despair prominent. Somatic symptoms were multiple. Their lives seemed not to make sense. Sanders suggests that most of the parents "gave the appearance of individuals who have suffered a physical blow which left them with no strength or will to fight." Losing a child of any age can be one of life's most devastating losses and its impact lingers for years—if not forever. Such a loss may alter the course of the parents' life and often of the parent's relationship to one another. Although the child's physical dependence on the parents lessens with age there may still be intense emotional dependence of one upon the other. In losing the child, the parent loses not only the relationship but a part of the self and a hope for the future.

Many children die in accidents, which heightens the challenge to the parent's sense of competency—their role to keep the children safe. Motor vehicle accidents are likely to involve other family members in many instances, unless the child is hit as a pedestrian. The shocking unexpected nature of these deaths lead to great problems of adjustment which will be heightened if the parent was in any way involved. If the mother or father was driving the car in which the child was killed or, as sometimes happens, backed the car out of the garage over the young child, guilt and blame are overwhelming. Blame from the other parent and family members is also very great.

About one million women a year in the United States alone suffer an unsuccessful pregnancy. People often fail to realize that a miscarriage or a stillbirth is a tragedy for a woman and one she remembers— perhaps all her life. One mother recalls her miscarriage and especially remembers the stillborn baby that was alive into the ninth month and was born weighing 13 pounds. She carried it dead inside her for the last two weeks. She said: "To give birth to a dead baby is a terrible thing for a mother." Her reaction is not always understood, even by other women. A woman who lost her child by miscarriage wrote: "What I have learned in a most painful way was that before this happened to me, I really had no idea of what my friends had to bear. I had been as insensitive and ignorant toward them as I now feel people are to me." Another problem for the grieving mother in this scenario is the impression that her husband may not feel the loss as she does. One wife reports how totally disappointed she was in her husband at the time. As far as the husband was concerned, there really was no pregnancy. He could not experience the grief that his wife was going through. He was very sympathetic to her fears but not to her grief. This reaction is natural for a husband—he does not undergo the same physical and emotional bonding that his pregnant wife does. Nevertheless, he suffers a loss. And it is vital that husband and wife realize that they are suffering together, although in different ways.

Although both parents have sustained a loss, the grief experience can be different for each due to their relationship with the child and their own coping styles. Men and women grieve differently and these differences can put a strain on a marital relationship, as well as other family members. The anticipated ideal of each spouse supporting and helping the other is rarely realized in the death of a child. Overwhelmed with grief, neither husband nor wife is in a position to be leaned upon. Do not expect that your spouse will understand completely or solve your grief—each has a special path of grief to follow. Share your grief. Share your tears, thoughts, and embraces. Show you need each other as never before. Often one spouse, or both, cannot seem to talk about the child. Scheduling a certain time for such talk has been the answer for many. At least the silent parent can listen during those periods and may talk eventually. Communication in general needs to continue. Do not harbor little grievances. Talk about them before they fester inside you.

Grieving the loss of a child may become even more complicated when the parents of the child are divorced. Parents are often brought together in a time of crisis and this coming together can evoke strong emotions and extreme behaviors, from empathy and compassion to power and control.

As in the death of other family members, the various tasks of mourning need to be worked through. For many parents who have lost children, the reality of the loss is a struggle of belief/disbelief. They know the child is gone but they don't want to believe it—they are supposed to outlive their children. When the parents do not see the body, the death may be even more unreal. Extreme anger about the accident—a hatred of the driver of the car or a desire to get revenge— may dominate the parents' response. Dealing with the child's belongings is a reflection of this struggle. Often parents will keep a child's room intact for many years after the death. The child is not forgotten and is always counted as one of the children.

WHEN A SIBLING DIES

Marion

My sister was twelve years of age—four years my senior. She was always a good girl and well-behaved. She made good grades in school. One day she decided to put on roller skates and go out to play. Not long after, she fell and hit her spine on the curb. When she came home, she complained of not feeling well. The following day she was worse. After visiting the doctor she was diagnosed with spinal meningitis. Two days later she died. It was so sudden and shocking and she was so young. I missed my sister not being around. One day she was a happy little girl playing and the next day she was dead.

— Harry Karcher

Charlie

At age twenty-nine, my brother, Charlie, went out to dinner with his friend. Charlie was bright, good-looking, energetic, and always on the run. So when he decided not to stay home for dinner, it wasn't unusual. However, he never came home that night. My parents woke up to every parent's nightmare. About 2:30 A.M. two police officers knocked on their door. I was called about 2:45 A.M. I woke up to an unfamiliar, monotone voice on my answering machine. I quickly grabbed the phone and heard a voice introducing himself as a police officer. He asked if I lived close to my parent's house. I said "yes" and then he asked me to please come there. I was shaking at this time but afraid to ask why. I just agreed to go. My father got on the phone at that time and again I was asked to please come over without any explanation. By now, I was in a panic. My heart was racing, my hands were shaking, and my head was spinning. I thought something happened to my mother. I couldn't understand why she didn't get on the phone. She was always the strong one in the family. My boyfriend had stayed over that night. Thank God, because I don't know how I would have been able to drive. Half way there, it hit me, "Oh, my God, Charlie." I was rocking back and forth in the passenger seat. I had realized it was 3:00 A.M. and who else would be out at this hour. For some reason, I knew it was a car accident. As we turned the corner, I was looking for his car. I remember saying, "Where's his car. Where's his car?" I ran into the house to find my mother sitting in a corner, curled up, rocking and hysterically crying. She kept saying. "No, not my Charlie," over and over and over. At that moment, I felt as if a knife went into my chest and took out my heart. The pain I was feeling is unimaginable! My father, who is six feet tall and weighed more than 200 pounds, looked so frail. Within minutes two of my other brothers arrived. There were six of us. The other two lived in Florida. So now the phone calls began. I started with my younger brother, who then had to tell our sister. I'll never forget the wailing I heard as I told the horrifying news to family and friends. My body was numb, my head in a fog, and my heart just raced on as if it was going to come through my chest. It was impossible to stop the tears. I couldn't believe he was gone. It was a living nightmare. And, as if losing my brother wasn't painful enough, I was now watching my parents suffer the loss of their son. They were like walking zombies. They aged ten years in ten minutes. As time went on, I remember being angry. I couldn't understand how life just continued. My brother was dead at twenty-nine and the world had the nerve to live on. I would feel guilty when I was finally able to laugh again. I have to say the first year after Charlie's death is hard to even remember. I think we all just carried on because we had no choice. The world does not stop even though we would have liked it to. My life changed after Charlie died. It changed the way I think, act, and do. I learned the hard way that life is too short. I realized how important it is to do the things I want to do. I learned what things in life are worth my energy and what things are so minute and not worth wasting energy on. I know now that until you experience something that someone else has you really don't know how they feel. One of the only things I found comforting was when someone else shared with me the loss of their sibling or their child. Nothing else could compare. Looking at my mother deteriorate after my brother died was almost as painful as dealing with his death. She never recovered from it. She and Charlie had a very special relationship. And, now two and a half years later, my mother and brother are together again. However, my mother didn't die suddenly. She had cancer throughout her body and suffered the last six months. It was easier to let her go knowing she doesn't have to suffer and now she can be with her Charlie again. I often wonder if the pain of losing my brother so suddenly will ever go away. I now have two holes in my heart—one for Charlie and one for Mom. Charlie's death has prepared me to deal with anything life has to offer. I feel that if I survived this nightmare, I can survive anything. There is not one day that goes by that I don't think of him and now my mother is in these thoughts also. I will never forget them.

— Margie

Robyn

In 1991, on September 24th, I experienced another trauma. I sat in a room full of support people. I shared that no matter what my higher power would put in my path, I would be able to handle. This was at 8:30 P.M. I left my safe meeting place and went home. Later, I went to bed, and in the still of the night the phone rang. I normally don't answer the phone. I would leave it for my husband because I always felt if anyone calls that late it would only be bad news. However, I answered it. On the other end I was asked if I was who I was. I stated yes. Then this cold and uncaring voice proceeded to tell me that my sister, Robyn, was in Beth Israel Hospital in Manhattan on a respirator and that she was going to die. However, the police needed to talk to me being I was the closest kin. I wrote all the information down in total shock. The woman continued to tell me that my sister was a terrible person and she overdosed on the city streets. She then stated if I didn't get in touch with the police that, when she did die, they would bury her as Jane Doe in Potter's Field. Totally confused, dazed, and all alone, I looked at the phone and said, "Enough." It's bad enough I might be losing the only person in my whole world that loved me unconditionally all my life, I didn't need this person to bad mouth her. I sat on my stairs all alone feeling once again in a cloud. I waited five hours before going to my parent's home to tell them the horrible news. We all jumped in the car and to the Manhattan hospital we went. We went into Robyn's room. Being I worked for a hospice I have seen dying people often. However, this case was so different. I felt in my heart Robyn's soul was not in her body. I couldn't even touch her. So unlike me. I've always been able to touch the living and the dead. However, not my sister, Robyn. I went home that day not believing what I saw nor what the doctor had said. He told me the machine was keeping her alive and that her body was going back into a fetal position. I, in mind, body, and soul, could not believe what I was going through once again. It was amazing that I was still breathing. How much could a person take? I went back to the hospital the following day. This time the curtains were closed. Right away the denial of the mind was that they were cleaning Robyn. As I went toward the curtain, I was asked to step into the hallway. I was with my parents and my husband. All of a sudden this woman doctor came past, stopped, looked as heartless as a person could look, and proceeded to tell me that my sister expired. I couldn't believe what I was hearing nor could I believe how coldly she was telling me. With this, my husband had gone to answer a call from my natural mother who left Robyn and me as infants. Here I was told Robyn was gone and my mother was on the phone at the exact time (she hadn't called in years). Then my husband comes out just as heartlessly as the doctor and tells me my natural mom wanted me to donate my sister's body to "SCIENCE" for one year. Then in a year they would give the body back and they would pay for the funeral. My head was spinning. How could my husband, the man who was to be there as my support, repeat such an evil thought? I just couldn't comprehend. That feeling of being in a cloud had reappeared. I needed to run, get away, and be by myself. So the doctor came back out, handed me a paper bag of Robyn's belongings which was nothing more than really dirty clothes (something Robyn was not all about). She always was a clean person who always looked great no matter what she wore. I took the bag and threw it in the nearby garbage. The doctor then stated I had to go to the city morgue to identify Robyn's body. The reason for this was that Robyn was thirty-five years of age and died on Manhattan streets and they needed to rule out foul play. Here again I couldn't believe what I was hearing and being my parents were my adopted parents, they were not considered close to kin, so I had to have the honors. I removed myself from everyone and sat in the stairwell and cried like a baby. The doctor went past and asked if they could do anything. Nicely I stated, "No"; however, in my head I wished they could make it all go away.

I went to the city morgue and there I looked at a picture of Robyn and was asked if this was her. "Yes," I replied. I brought Robyn home and gave her a beautiful funeral. I was even able to give her a eulogy. I stated how Robyn was out of pain and that she now was in a better place. However, I miss her each day and will always continue to miss her. She is still alive in my heart and I keep her alive within my children's hearts. We know that Robyn suffered from a terrible disease called Addiction.

— Patricia Puma

*   *   *

When a sibling dies, both parents and remaining children must adjust to a new reality. A complex family process begins. The family is involved in what is known as "survivor guilt"—a pain experienced by those who feel responsible in some way for the death of another. In the death of a sibling, the other siblings may feel their own guilt for having survived when their dead brother or sister did not. Sometimes this guilt is a result of the wish most children have about being the only child. If he or she was the only child, he or she would have all the attention from the parents. He or she would have more toys as well as other belongings. At some time during our childhood, most of us told our brother or sister to "drop dead." Although this is done only as a retort, we never expect them to really do it. When a death occurs, expectedly or unexpectedly, the remaining sibling is plagued with the awful memory of that or of similar retorts. Because of shame, it is generally internalized and kept secret for fear that others will think the worst—the worst being that they may have been the cause of the death. Emotions are repressed and the guilt is buried, often causing behavioral problems later in life. In other cases, siblings have guilt because they think the best or the nicest child has died. Unfortunately, the surviving sibling will believe they don't deserve to be alive.

Often, the child will try to duplicate the mood created by the parents. If the circumstances of the tragedy are clear, as in Marion's death, they are in a better position to honestly deal with their own emotions. If the circumstances are ambiguous and the atmosphere of the environment tense, then it will be difficult for the surviving child to separate his or her involvement in the situation.

The effect of such a close death may increase the surviving child's sense of vulnerability to death, especially when siblings are close to one another in age. There is often a mixture of emotions. For example, if the brother was a protector as well as a playmate, the sister may be sad that this relationship has ended—worried that the protection is no longer available and, at the same time, relieved now that the brother is gone because she can now be the center of attention. This mixture of emotions can create guilt and confusion in the surviving child.

Most of what is true for adults in grief also holds true for children. Like adults, children display a variety of reactions to the death of a loved one. They go through the same types of grief as long and intensely as their adult family members. They have many of the same needs as adults—many of the same symptoms and issues arise. Like adults, they experience shock, numbness, panic, disorganization, and despair. Unlike adults, however, they dart in and out of the chaos. Children suspect that the loss of a sibling will irrevocably alter the rest of their lives, and they are frightened by the powerful feelings accompanying this radical change.

Some people feel it is wiser to protect the child from death and to find ways in which to soften its impact. Yet all the available evidence suggests that not to assist the bereaved child in actively confronting the death is to predispose him to significant pathology and lifelong problems. The bereaved sibling must be given a chance to express his or her grief. Feelings of guilt and confusion, as well as sadness, need to be resolved in a loving and supportive atmosphere. Children usually cope more easily with their feelings about a close death or serious illness of a sister or brother when they are allowed to participate in the experience of grief and mourning. When they are excluded, or when their questions go unanswered, the resulting uncertainty in the child's mind produces additional anxiety, confusion, and pain. Sharing the reality of what is happening allows a child to begin to understand and cope with the experience.

The child who experiences a sudden death may need extra support in coping with the unanticipated grief response that results from an untimely and unexpected death. The child will need to get some sense of security again, something even adults have trouble with when such a death occurs.

My Brother, My Friend

He was there for me when I needed someone to listen.
He was there to cheer me up when I was down.
He was there when I needed a shoulder to lean on.
He was there through the good and the bad.
He cared about me and wasn't afraid to show it.
He was my best friend.

Michael Sten (David's brother)

WHEN OTHER SPECIAL PEOPLE DIE

Mary

The Dream—I went to bed late that night. It had been difficult to sleep since my mother-in-law had passed away. My husband, Gil, and I were still suffering the loss. I was trying to find a way to cope with so many unsettled feelings. I was not with her when she passed away. Gil had gone to New York alone to be with her, while I stayed home with our small children. And in my shock and sorrow, I had felt the incompleteness of our suddenly ended relationship.

Mary and I had experienced many disagreements in the past. Our different cultures and lifestyles made it hard for me to understand my mother-in-law at times. But it seemed we were finally making headway . . . becoming closer. I loved her, though I did not know if she had known it. And I could not lay her to rest.

But that night, I had a dream. It was incredibly strong. Mary was here, sitting on our couch. I came to her, with tears softly flowing down my face, as I spoke the words I longed to say . . . "I love you." "I know . . . ," Mary replied. She held me in her arms briefly as I wept at her knees, before she had to go. She told me she was going to see Gil.

I awoke immediately after the dream. Gil woke at the same moment. We both knew that Mary had been in one another's dreams. Her presence was felt. It is hard to explain the power which moved through us that night. But it was a divine power. One which gave us both comfort and peace.

— Lori Tegano

Lee

It all began about thirteen years ago. My father, John, a healthy strong active man, was diagnosed with cardio-myopathy, a weakening of the heart muscle. He ran the gamut of tests from EKGs to angiograms but was told by doctors that there was nothing they could do but prescribe medication. Lots of medication. He went on for several years, slowly getting weaker and weaker. He was becoming less of the strong dominant man I always admired, and was showing signs of vulnerability, something he never did as I was growing up. He stayed with us for about five years and then after having a stroke, gave up his will to live and passed on. That was five days after I returned home from my honeymoon and two weeks prior to his sixty-first birthday. Even though we had our differences, I always loved my father and aspired to be very much like him.

My father was one of the first persons that were close to me that passed away. His death was the beginning of a string of deaths within my family. Within six months, my husband's uncle died. Six months after that, my grandmother passed away. I was becoming numb!

No one could replace the void in my heart that my father's death had left, but I was growing closer to my new father-in-law, and it felt good. We laughed together, he was supportive of my crazy idea, and I know he loved me just as much as I loved him. I was just getting to know him—and then he was gone!

It was so sudden, his death, but it was exactly the way he wanted to go. My father-in-law was a man who feared illness and death; he would never even participate in conversations about a loved one who was ill and in the hospital. That is how much he could not deal with the whole idea. He had always told my mother-in-law that when his time came he wished it to be swift and while playing racquetball with his buddies. This sport was one of his greatest joys. On the last day in March 1993, my father-in-law had a massive coronary while in mid-swing while playing racquetball with his friends. He was dead before he hit the ground. It was just the way he wanted it to be.

The numbness of my own father's death slipped away briefly so that I could feel the hurt and pain all over again with my father-in-law's death. I cried, I still cry, I cried a lot as I've been writing this story. Some of the differences between my father's and father-in-law's deaths are that although you never quite get used to the idea, I did have the opportunity to somewhat prepare myself for my father's death. The swiftness of my father-in-law's death didn't even allow for a last hug and kiss good-bye. Being of different religions, my husband's family and mine, funeral proceedings were contrasted. During the wake of my father I was able to see and accept that he was dead and had the opportunity to say good-bye and I love you. Being of the Jewish faith, my father-in-law was buried the next day, the casket was closed at his funeral and I never had the chance to see him again, to say I love you and I'll miss you. There was no closure.

To this day, there still is no closure. And the numbness has set in once more.

— Janine Rego-Rosen

Archie

I am currently mourning the death of a dear sweet friend of mine. Archie was a light-heavyweight boxing champion for twelve years during the '50s and '60s. I met him in 1974 in San Diego, California, through his son, Billy. I had played professional football in the Continental Professional Football league and Billy was my roomate. We became great friends. We didn't make a lot of money, but we had a good time and enjoyed each others friendship. I had family living in San Diego and so, after the season was over and the team disbanded, Billy asked me to come to California and I said, "Sure, why not?" I met Billy's father and we hit it off immediately. I even lived with them for awhile on the family estate. Archie and I played pool together and listened to jazz for hours. He also gave me free boxing lessons for about a year. I didn't know that, in the mid '90s, he lost his son, Hardy, to an incurable disease. I was shocked and surprised when Billy told me about it since I did not even know he was sick. I hadn't talked to Billy in about three or four years so I didn't know. Also, I didn't know that Archie, whom I called Pops, had gone through major heart surgery a couple of years ago. Then, in December, I was looking at ESPN and sad news is announced on the program—light-heavyweight boxing champion Archie Moore has died. I was hurt and sad. My friend, Pops, was gone.

— Larry D. Jennings

Angel Christopher

The life of one person cannot be
measured in time.
The impact of a life cut so short
should be shared with all
so we can help those left behind heal
their broken hearts.
Time will be what is needed now
to remember Christopher—
as a son, brother, grandson,
nephew, cousin, student, friend.
Christopher was a special someone
to each and every one of us.

His memory will be with us for
always.
Each one of us has been touched in
someway by Christopher.
His rosy cheeks that held the
laughter of a happy child.
His courage as a fighter
or his hidden strength for someone
so young.
A life taken from us much too soon.
When we remember Christopher
these thoughts come to mind.
We should be thankful for the time
that Christopher blessed our lives
and know he is at peace now . . .
And forever in our thoughts and in
our hearts.

— Written and read by Tina Chlibun (cousin)
Contributed by Ron and Maria Faller

Gracia

I recently lost my very best friend in all the world. We have been best friends and confidantes for almost forty years. In fact, we were so close that, no matter how far apart we were, we telecommunicated.

I had just had a very happy two-day, pre-Christmas visit with my grandchildren and was anxious to get home so I could call Gracia and tell her all about the visit. Upon arriving home, my husband told me he had some bad news for me. My mind was spinning through the possibilities—the cat? (she is 20 years old) . . . my son? (a police officer) . . . my mom? . . . my dad? (both up in their years). He assured me that the cat and my son were okay and proceeded to start holding me very close, as he told me Gracia had died the previous morning. I was in complete shock. "No!!! I don't believe it!!! She was coming to visit for a month or two in February. We already had the money set aside for her plane tickets!!! She can't be dead!!!" Tears began to flow, my heart was torn, my soul felt like it left my body. I had never felt such agonistic pain in my life.

Now, it is three months later, and I still mourn deeply for Gracia. A day doesn't go by that I don't shed a tear for the loss of my very dear friend. It was so sudden and unexpected. I fight the depression and try to keep on with life. But, I can see, and feel, that the usual aggression in accomplishing tasks has disappeared. I procrastinate more and cry quite often. I know she is with the angels and has no more pain. My grief is purely selfish because she isn't here in the flesh. I feel like she has deserted me. The plans and dreams we had . . . so close to our goal . . . just to have her die. Things left undone.

— Sandi B.

Kyle

You'll Never Be Forgotten
That night when I heard the phone ring,
In my head I heard angels sing.
I just cried and cried.
I was hurt and confused inside.
I knew you were traveling that long journey
Between my world and yours.
I knew you were going to a much better place.
I knew they would treat you with lots of love and care.
I knew you would find your lost loved ones there.
I know I will reunite with you up there in heaven.
What I don't know is how soon and when.
Your spirit will for once be free, but there will always
Be an empty space inside of me.
You're gone from my view, but not from my heart.
And until you're forgotten, we'll never be apart.
Why does life have to end so fast?
I'm just glad I've got memories that last.
I miss all the songs we used to sing.
I miss visiting you.
I miss everything.
I'll never forget you and our memories.
All I have to ask of you is,
Don't forget me, please!
I'll always remember the support I gave and the advice I received.
I'll never forget the happiness we achieved.
Your voice will never leave my mind—
How it was so smooth and soft as cotton.
Just, please, always remember,
No one is dead until they are forgotten.
I will always miss you, Kyle.

— your friend, Jennifer Glick, age 14

*   *   *

Just as the death of a loved family member is a painful experience, so is the death of a friend or other special people in our life. Friends are extremely important at any stage of the life cycle. The death of a friend can be not only a profound personal loss but a deeply disturbing one. One example of this type of loss is what our country has been experiencing with school shootings. Sadly enough, these deaths have included siblings as well as friends but, surprisingly, little attention has been given to the death of an adolescent's friend—or to experiences of bereaved adolescent parents. More research needs to be addressed in these areas.

Studies have shown that bereavement during adolescence does not necessarily predispose one to psychological difficulties. In fact, it may actually help many adolescents to become more emotionally and interpersonally mature (Fleming & Balmer, 1996, p. 153). However, the death of a friend is extremely difficult to deal with at such a young age. Much can be done to help bereaved adolescents cope when a friend dies. Provide them with information about loss and begin the process of interpreting and integrating that loss into their lives. Teach them how to express their feelings in safe and manageable ways—finding their own way of coping. Include them in funeral practices and memorial services. Help them find ways to go on with their lives in a healthy and productive manner. Provide counseling when necessary and establish a group of bereaved peers. Encourage them to talk. Be prepared to listen!

Another death which may be difficult to deal with is that of a co-worker. When a co-worker dies, your productivity and the dynamics of your workplace are affected. You may have spent many hours with the person and consider him a friend, not just a co-worker. People who work together are like extended families.

Other deaths include a teacher, a neighbor, or even a patient. For example, staff members of a long-term health care facility may become very much attached to the people in their care. An elderly woman with no living relatives may be considered adopted by a nurse who takes care of her on a daily basis. Our society usually acknowledges the right of a caregiver to grieve. The bereaved nurse who is not bestowed the right to mourn must find some other way to deal with the stress, which may lead to physical and emotional problems.

Help me up my friend.
Dust me off.
Feed me warmth.
You are comfort.
Let me lean on you until I can stand alone.
I will then stand a little taller.
And you will be proud to have a friend such as I.
— Author Unknown

WHEN A PET DIES

Nutmeg

Nutmeg, or as we affectionately called her, "Nutty," died suddenly on Monday, January 4th. She was fourteen years old and had been a joy to all the family members, but especially to my grandson, Ryan, age nine. She was his constant companion from the day he came home from the hospital. I referred to her as my granddog and loved her very much as did everyone who had been in contact with her. She would greet you at the front door with a stuffed animal in her mouth and her tail would wag until you made a big fuss over her—petting her and calling her name. And then, Nutty had a massive heart attack without warning on that fateful day. My son-in-law, John, took her to the vet who put Nutty to rest. Ryan cried when he was told that she died and the next day he made plans to bury her collar and leash, her favorite stuffed animal, and her dog food. About a week later, while visiting, I asked Ryan how he felt about not having Nutty anymore. He waited for a moment and then said to me, "You know, Grandma, just because Nutty is dead doesn't mean she isn't here anymore. I see her on my bed and sometimes I feel her nudge my leg and so I pet her. She will always be with me."

— Geri Brogan

Pal

This story starts one day in 1970 when I walked into a bide-a-wee home for animals. I wanted to adopt a dog. I had my heart set on a German Shepherd. I passed this cage a couple of times and this little puppy kept following me as far as his cage would let him, with this "take me" look in his eyes. He was a beagle about eight weeks old. I did not want any sissy little dog. I wanted a great big attack dog to protect my family. Well, I ended up adopting him. I do not remember how I picked the name, but Pal it was.

I remember him chewing up a couch and a few pairs of shoes, but on the whole he was a good dog and very smart. I did not spend a lot of time teaching him tricks but he learned right away the tone in my voice when I told him to sit and stay and called him to my side, he listened. Pal seemed to want to do something for me all of the time. There was really nothing for him to do but hang around and eat and sleep. When my first son was born, Pal took to him very well even though my son would drop his Fisher Price toys out of the play pen on Pal's head. Then he started walking and would pull everything Pal had to be pulled, but his temperament was remarkable. Pal never once showed signs of aggression. I remember also when strangers would come around and he would start barking and I would say to him, one time, "down" and he would listen but he would never take his eyes off that person. I found out later that he was a mix of shepherd and beagle. If he liked you, he loved you to death but if he did not like you, he wanted to tear your heart out. The only thing I had going for me was the fact my voice would stop him in his tracks.

When we moved out to the suburbs he sort of felt more in his environment and loved to chase things through the woods. One day he found a rabbit in the woods and chased him for an hour until he gave up from being exhausted. A little while later there were two rabbits and they used to wait for him outside the back door in the morning and they would lead the chase for quite a while. Pal used to wait by the side of my bed in the morning, waiting for me to move and then stick his cold nose in my face. I know what he wanted, and he knew not to wake me until I showed some sign of being conscious. We went through that lesson one time when he jumped on me in my sleep, and he learned real fast not to ever do that again. So down to the back door we went and there were the rabbits waiting for Pal. This went on for a lot of years until one day in 1985, Christmas Eve to be exact, I let him out and that was the last time I saw him alive. I knew his sight and hearing was less acute the last few years because of his age, but he always seemed to know where the back door was and would let me know when he wanted to come in, except this time he must have lost his sense of direction and ended up out in the street where a car hit and killed him instantly. I found him right outside my driveway with my son. I remember how sick I felt and my son crying and holding Pal. I never thought that Pal would die that way. I always thought he would get old and die, but now that I think back, dying is so final and our reaction to it would have probably been the same. My son and I picked up Pal and we buried him in the back yard. There is a bush and flowers where he is buried and I think about my Pal every day. The two rabbits, they waited for him for a couple of weeks after that. I guess they missed him too!

— Joseph Gruttola

*   *   *

As a grief counselor, I believe pet loss is an area that is often overlooked in grief assessment. It is also neglected as a learning opportunity for teaching children about their first death experience. By opportunity, I mean it can be the event that initiates a healthy, open, and loving relationship of living and dying, or it can be the event that initiates an unhealthy, dishonest approach to living and dying. When a pet dies, parents may wonder how best to help their child cope with the loss. Should one try to minimize the child's loss? Or should the death be seen as a natural opportunity for the child to consider what death means and to explore her feelings about the loss? For many, the loss of a pet cannot be equated to that of a human life, but it is a devastating experience for the child, elderly person living alone, or childless couple. It is true that one cannot compare animal and human death. The losses are different and cannot be adequately measured. What is important is the relationship with the one that has died—whether they are made of flesh or fur. The bond that attaches people to their pet is often extremely strong—a loyal relationship based on unconditional love.

In my profession, I have read a lot of literature, listened to many people, participated in numerous discussions concerning the topic of death. I have suffered the loss of many family members and friends. Each and every time a beloved pet dies, I experience the pain over and over again. All previous losses seem to surface each time I grieve.

I am truly amazed when people apologize for being upset when their pet dies. Attachments between humans and pets can be very strong. Yet mourning the loss of a pet sometimes elicits ridicule. Some may say that the bereaved pet owner is overreacting. Those who counsel individuals who are grieving over the loss of a pet emphasize that feelings should be expressed by adults as well as children. We grieve for our family and friends when they die so why not our pets? After all, they amuse us and comfort us and occasionally annoy us. Pets are always there for us, to protect us from harm and to teach us the true meaning of loyalty and love. In turn, they only expect to be fed, cared for, and loved. When they die, or disappear, we need to express all the sadness and grief we feel inside.

As for replacing a pet, sufficient time should be allowed to mourn the loss before a new animal is acquired. This may take weeks or months—perhaps even longer. The bonds of attachment to the pet that has died may jeopardize a healthy transition of affection to another animal if the natural process of grief has been prematurely curtailed or ignored.

Unfortunately, there are not enough people who can understand our grief. Those of us who mourn the death of a pet are usually more generous and empathetic in our expressions of care and concern for others. Too often those we rely on most let us down during our grief simply because they do not understand. We may be fortunate to find other caring and supportive people who have pets of their own and who can share our feelings and sadness.

Very little is published in the media regarding this subject because death is still a taboo subject in our society. Below are some suggestions after the loss of a beloved pet:

- Express your feelings. Don't hold back the tears. If you suppress these feelings, it will only delay the grief process.
- Make a donation or dedication to a worthy cause in your pet's memory.
- Remove toys and other things that remind you of your pet. Seeing them will only intensify your grief and make your recovery more difficult.
- If you find it necessary, hold a private service or memorial for your beloved pet. If you have children, they should be involved. This is an excellent beginning in teaching your child about death.
- Keep a daily journal listing your major thoughts and feelings.
- Write a letter to your pet. You will be amazed at how therapeutic this activity can be. You may even want to write a letter or Last Will and Testament from your pet to yourself. Keep this as a memory for some time in the future.
- Avoid situations that may be upsetting (e.g., going for a walk if you did this with your pet or spending time with non-pet lovers).
- If you live alone, try to make slight changes in daily activities (e.g., go to the library or meet with an old friend who loved your pet).
- Watch a funny movie or television show or read a humorous and entertaining book.
- Contact your clergyman or locate a counselor who can give you therapeutic advice.
- If loneliness pervades, get another furry companion—not to replace your beloved pet, but to add comfort to your life with a new friend.

If you choose to bury your pet, there are many very good and distinguished pet cemeteries widely located throughout the United States. For more information on what is available in your area, it is best to ask your local veterinarian, as well as other pet owners who have used these facilities.

All pet lovers will someday face the death of their furry friend. The information here has been provided to make that time in your life easier to deal with.

PART TWO

Grief Work

CHAPTER 2

Recovery and Growth

It has been fifteen years since Leo died and I would like to share with you my adjustment to, and the beginning of, a new life. Most of this book, prior to this point, was written on and off during the first six years after Leo's death. It was difficult to begin but, overall, has been a very therapeutic experience for me. At times I would have to stop writing and go to Paul for a hug just to get back in touch with reality. Reading and editing the first half of this book brought back many memories as well as tears. I learned a lot about myself. I understand my strengths and my weaknesses.

In 1986, I married Paul—a wonderful man with two daughters. We have a great marriage—one in which we allow one another space to grow and be ourselves. Paul stood by me during those trying times. He was understanding and had the patience of a saint.

In 1989, I returned to school and, in the last seven years, I received a bachelor's degree in Community Health, a master's degree in Community Mental Health Counseling, and a doctorate in Human Services Administration.

My daughter, Natalie, is now twenty-three years old. She works and goes to school and is doing well.

I have come a long way since Leo's death. My travels through grief gave me the inspiration and ambition to do something with my life. For this I am thankful and would like to share my ideas and suggestions with you. Remember—grief is unique and it affects each one of us in an individual way.

> To grieve well is to value what you have lost. When you value even the feeling of loss, you value life itself, and you begin to live again (Frank, 1991, p. 41).

THREE STAGES OF GRIEF

Grief is the term used to describe the psychological and physiological reactions you are experiencing—the things that are happening now in your mind and body. Grief is not a disease. You cannot wave a magic wand and make it disappear. It is a long, agonizing process, but fortunately it does have an end. Not everyone experiences the same feelings at the same points in time. Grief is usually experienced in three distinct stages and each stage must be gone through completely before you can feel normal again.

Numbness

The first stage of grief begins at the moment of death, and continues for the next several weeks or months. If you are lucky, during this time you have friends and neighbors who are concerned about your welfare. They are there to be leaned upon, physically and emotionally. You may be surprised to notice that you keep an emotional distance from these people. That is because you are not ready to deal with all your innermost feelings. You must perform certain tasks, such as funeral arrangements or estate settlements, which need your immediate attention. Your functioning may be automatic, mechanical, and robot-like. That is because you are still numb from the shock of the death. You may feel as if you are suspended in an unreal state. During this stage of grief you may feel as if you are in a bad dream which will soon be over. This is your mind's way of protecting you from really feeling the painful finality of death.

One emotion which occasionally surfaces at this early stage, besides sorrow, is a feeling of anger toward the deceased. Soon after, guilt takes over and neutralizes that anger, which may show up again during the next phase of the grief process. When someone you love dies,

> When the husbands' death is sudden and totally unexpected, the widow's shock and numbness are likely to be pervasive. She has not had time to say goodbye, to think about being alone, or to make even the most rudimentary and tentative plans (Silverman, 1986, p. 34).

Disorganization

The second or middle phase of grief begins as soon as the shock starts to wear off. Several weeks or months have passed since the death. Friends and family have resumed their prior commitments and are not as attentive as they once were. Your neighbor, who usually checked in each day to see how you were doing, now comes by only once a week. The relatives who used to telephone regularly now just write occasionally. Everyone is back into their regular routine. It seems that, for everyone else, life has returned to what it was before the death. It is ironic and sad that now, when you can finally appreciate those people and no longer want or need to feel distant from others, there is no one there to share your feelings. The numbness subsides and the full meaning of the loss is felt. There is severe loneliness and emptiness where there was once life. These feelings are normal during this stage of grief.

Friends and relatives may become alarmed at the way you are acting. They don't realize that a disorganization of personality, including symptoms of depression, is to be expected now. Aimlessness and apathy, loss of appetite and loss of sleep, constant crying, are all indications of the pain you feel. Other symptoms of grief include feelings of tightness in the throat, shortness of breath, the need to frequently sigh, and extreme fatigue. You may feel restless and cannot concentrate. This could be because you have not yet fully accepted your loss as a permanent situation. The urge to find your lost one, your yearning and your hope, bring on feelings of anxiety and panic. Gradually, as reality emerges, you will give up hoping for that reunion and begin accepting and adjusting. This may not make you feel better because, while the anxiety you felt was a reaction to the danger of a loss, the increasing awareness of the loss brings pain.

During this stage you are feeling a persistent pain of loneliness and at the same time are being confronted with new responsibilities. Whether it is paying the bills, taking out the garbage, or running errands, you are doing chores that were once someone else's obligation. Each of these is now a reminder of the person's death.

Objects belonging to the deceased may take on particular emotional significance. When you were little and had to be separated from your mother, you had a comforting reminder of her to carry around while she was away. Such reminders are called transitional objects by professionals, but are more remembered as "security blankets." You may be using a transitional object now to remind you of your lost loved one. Most people do need some articles of the deceased which they may sleep with, wear, hold, or just look at. This is normal behavior for this stage of grief.

Now as you experience the pain of deep feelings you may be resentful and feel sorry for yourself. This, too, is normal. Feeling sorry for yourself is a major part of grief work. It is necessary for you to feel sorry for yourself and for your predicament. Other emotions during the middle stage of grief are shame, fear, guilt, hopelessness and helplessness, and anger. Feelings of anger that were brief during the initial stage will more than likely recur with greater frequency and strength. Your anger should not be hidden by those attempting to help you. Even rage is appropriate at this point. If you hide from the anger you feel toward the deceased you may develop symptoms at a later date—symptoms which may be far more difficult to deal with than the original anger. It is normal to feel angry. You were abandoned by someone you love. These feelings of anger are proof that you are human. Many people in this situation are embarrassed to notice that they are hostile in the presence of those same people who are trying to help. This occurs often, but eventually your hostility will disappear. In the meantime, it is a normal reaction and you should not hide or deny it—just let it happen.

> Even after we recover from the initial shock of loss, there will be times in the coming days and months when we again feel "I can't believe it!" Our psyches scrutinize the actuality of death over and over, attempting to accept and integrate the loss into our lives. Because death is usually a fact we do not want to believe, it is a long, slow process to overcome our resistance and accept reality. The truth is that we keep hoping we will awaken from this nightmare (Tatelbaum, 1984, p. 27).

In close relationships there is always the chance of shouting, yelling, feeling resentful, or even saying "Drop dead" or "I hope you never come back." While normal human beings are capable of anger, they do not have magical powers. Anger cannot kill. Guilt feelings must be expressed in order for you to experience what you already know on an intellectual level—that the death did not occur because of your wishing so. Unresolved guilt is a basic problem of grief. Whatever loss you feel is real, regardless of the superficial quality of the relationship. Even the occasional harsh words you had with the deceased are proof of the intimacy you shared. We do not argue with strangers. We care enough to pursue issues only with people with whom we are closely associated. The husband who fought furiously with his wife is in the same pain, and going through the same grief as the husband who showed kindness toward his wife. The daughter grieving for the mother with whom she argued on a daily basis is suffering as much as the daughter who never disagreed with her parents.

Acknowledging the negative as well as the positive traits of the deceased will help you get through grief at a steady pace.

You cannot prevent the hands of sorrow from flying over your head, but you can prevent them from building a nest in your hair (Chinese proverb).

Setbacks in the process occur when you are unable to recognize those parts of the deceased person's personalities which were disagreeable to you. It is difficult to handle these painful emotions. In fact, getting through the stages of grief is hard work. It is called grief work, and grief work is the emotional reorganization you must deal with before life can return to normal again.

During this middle stage of grief, you may forget that the person you loved is really gone for good. This is normal behavior. A new widow who, for many years, has set a dinner table for two, may still continue to do so. The widower who hears the telephone ring, may automatically ask his wife to answer it.

It is normal to occasionally act as if the dead person is still alive. Bereaved people will sometimes hallucinate during this state. The wife wants so much to hear the familiar sounds indicating that her husband has returned from work that she is certain she hears the car pulling into the driveway or his key turning in the lock.

> The bereaved become intensely preoccupied with the deceased. "I am completely occupied by him!" "I am so full of him." "I wish that I could get my mind off him." At the same time the bereaved may take on symptoms, mannerisms, habits or personality traits of the deceased. "Sometimes when I am speaking, I do not know whether it is he or me." He yearns and pines for the deceased, walks about restlessly, as if searching for her, sees people whom, for an instant, he mistakes for the deceased, and sometimes calls out her name (Silverman, 1986, p. 4).

Many bereaved people look forward to dreams that let them be with the deceased. Reports of ghosts, haunted houses, and footsteps in the night, as well as some evidence of successful seances, may be attributed to the urgent wish to be in contact with the deceased. Hallucinations give a sense of presence and help maintain the feeling that your loved one is nearby.

You may now have a need to talk about your feelings. You may also have a need to talk about the life and the death of your loved one. As you pass through this troubled time, it becomes psychologically necessary to review the details of the life you shared with the deceased. Whether or not the people around you consider it necessary, it is extremely important that you are encouraged to speak of the past. Eventually you will go on to other things—like talking about the actual death. It may be necessary for you to discuss over and over every last detail. You should always feel free to talk about the circumstances of the death. In order to process the finality of the situation you need to relive those last few days or hours. By going over the details of the death, you finally recognize the reality of the situation.

Symptoms of the middle stage of grief closely resemble some symptoms of mental illness. The difference is that indications of mental illness do not spontaneously and permanently disappear, while indications of grief will disappear as the mourning process is completed.

The famous actress Helen Hayes commented on her adjustment to widowhood by saying

> For two years I was just as crazy as you can be, and still be at large. I didn't have any really normal minutes during those two years. It wasn't just grief. It was total confusion. How did I come out of it? I don't know, because I didn't know when I was in it, that I was in it (Caine, 1974, pp. 75-76).

Lynn Caine, after the death of her husband, states

> I didn't know I was in it either; all I knew was that I hurt. But looking back, I was certainly a crazy lady. Oh, I thought I was eminently sane, that I was making wise decisions. But I was acting like an idiot (Caine, 1974, p. 76).

Caine describes her inability to be at peace with herself during the mid-stage of grief. She stated, "I had to do something." That, of course, is the trap most widows fall into. The most difficult advice in the world to follow is "Do nothing."

In an effort to be helpful to you, some people may respond to your grief symptoms as if they were symptoms of several mental illnesses. It is important for you to know and remind yourself that you were not mentally ill prior to the death of your loved one and that you will recover from grief and regain your ability to function. Bereavement happens to an existing personality. You have strengths, weaknesses, and previous experiences of coping with loss. To cope is to acknowledge that a problem exists and then to decide upon a course of action. The combination of your personality structure, the intelligence of the people available to you, and time itself will determine how rocky or smooth the road through grief will be.

Reorganization

Middle-stage mourners find the complexity of life threatening and frightening. Daily chores are too much to handle. But as you pass through the mid-stage of grief, you again find the world a rewarding and secure place.

The double task of mourning—completion of the emotional relationship with the deceased and redirecting energy toward the future—usually begins to be accomplished somewhere between the first and second anniversary of the death. You cry less and the need to talk about the deceased diminishes. Sleep and appetite eventually become normal again. You may be surprised to find that occasionally several hours, and maybe even a full day, might pass during which your mind does not automatically return to thoughts of the deceased. Now when you awake, the first thought of the day is not necessarily of the deceased, but of the day's activities. This end-stage of mourning is a relief. Life is no longer one frantic anxiety attack. There is a commitment to the future—you know that the dead person will never be forgotten and you also know that your life will continue.

Try Again

I'm tired of gloom;
I'm tired of pain;
I want to rejoin
The world again.

Life does proceed
When a loved one leaves
But it's difficult for me
Who is left to grieve.

Today I will try
To smile once more.
Death disappeared
And left my door.

I'll pick myself up
And try again;
I'll make the effort
To function again.

It won't be easy
As I well know,
But I won't give up
The change made me grow.

I loved him so much,
And fate was unkind.
He went away first;
He left me behind.

The pain in my heart
Will remain for a while
But yesterday's gone
Today I will smile.
                                   Anonymous Author
                                   Newsday, Long Island, 1984

You may be lucky to have someone in your present life who is able to acknowledge a signal that lets them know they are welcome to be a part of your future. A telephone call, a question about a future meeting or event, a tentative plan—all these should be encouraged by the helping friend or relative. The people helping you have chores to perform during each stage of grief. During stage one of the grief process, the person is there to be leaned upon and give assistance with managing necessary chores. During stage two the person must provide the space for you to express emotions, all emotions, and must tirelessly listen to the repeated stories about the life and death of the loved one. In the last stage of grief, this person must be there to help you interact socially and encourage involvement and interest in life.

> The widow in our society suffers not only from the pain associated with her loss, but also from the lack of rituals that guide her through mourning, help her understand what is happening, facilitate the comfort offered by others, and help her reorganize her life in light of the many changes caused by her husband's death. These changes are largely associated with the loss of her role as wife and the need to find a new role (Silverman, 1986, p. 19).

At this point you have successfully completed mourning. You are feeling good once again. You care about yourself. You are reorganizing your life toward the future. You are calm, but you may still have terrible days. As time passes, the bad days will occur less frequently.

You must try not to be alarmed by occasional setbacks. Some people find that they may do well for a whole year and then find themselves totally devastated by grief on the anniversary of the death. Such anniversary reactions are normal. Silverman (1986) reported that some people who felt they had recovered completely from the pangs of grief might be engulfed in a wave of distress months or years later. Some of the diary entries expressed a more profound sense of grief years after the loss than they had at the time.

Judaic law has a prescribed ritual for "death days"—the anniversary of the death.

> Often the anticipation of this anniversary is worse than the actual day. Once it has passed you will have completed a whole year of first-time anniversaries, and the next time these occasions will probably be less painful and more enjoyable for you. At the same time, I would not want you to expect instant relief. I think you will find the pain subsiding, but it will be gradual and not immediate (Fitzgerald, 1994, p. 115).

The degree of grief one feels is in direct proportion to the depth of feeling one had before the loss. Everyone feels the separation, some more than others. Some feel anger, some guilt, some fear, some frustration. But real grief, the kind that shakes your whole being and feels as though you cannot possibly bear it, that is grief, not just loss.

> Grief is neither a disorder nor a healing process; it is a sign of health itself, a whole and natural gesture of love. Nor must we see grief as a step towards something better. No matter how much it hurts—and it may be the greatest pain in life—grief can be an end in itself, a pure expression of love (May, 1972, p. 3).

CONFRONTING GRIEF

The day will come, months or years later, when you accept the death of your loved one. You grieved for as long as you needed. Sadness will enter your life from time to time to remind you of your sorrow but now you are better prepared for it. Grief is sometimes harder to deal with months after the death because that is when you begin to face your problems.

In the beginning you can avoid grief but, eventually, it must be faced. If resisted, it simply goes deeper inside and surfaces as a physical problem or emotional distress. Grief happens at its own pace. It refuses to be rushed and does not ease pain until one has been completely drained.

Earlier I discussed three stages of grief that I researched by other professionals. Now looking back over my period of recovery, I realize I progressed through those stages of grief in a similar way but with a few changes here and there. I call my stages SAG—shock, adjustment, and growth.

Shock

In those first days following my husband's death, I behaved in a capable and efficient manner. I functioned well by making all the necessary arrangements and remained strong through each and everyone. From all outward appearances, I did what was expected of me. But today I can hardly remember the specifics of those days! It was my state of shock—not my inner strength—which allowed me to handle all I needed to at that time. It got me through the hours and the rituals. But, inside, there was a big hole. Nothing seemed real to me.

About a month later, everything changed. I was delirious—sobbing uncontrollably, angry at the world, and full of despair and rage, but most of all, guilt. The guilt I was feeling was overwhelming for several reasons. Shortly before Leo died, we were with friends and somehow the subject of death came up. A comment was made about whether a friend of ours would marry again since her husband had died. I said, "She's only 55—she may meet someone in time." Well, Leo was shocked and said to me, "Don't you get any such ideas. If I died and you remarried, I would turn in my grave!" Ironically, Leo died a two weeks later and two years after that I returned from my honeymoon only to end up in the emergency room with what was diagnosed as a "virus." After a spinal tap to determine if I had meningitis, I was sent home with a horrible headache. I made myself sick thinking about what I had done by getting married again. At this time I still had not gotten over having to make the decision about "pulling the plug" on the respirator and, to top that off, I was still feeling as if I had killed Leo by making love to him that night. I kept saying, "If only I hadn't, maybe he would still be alive."

Grief had taken over my heart, body, and soul. I was also affected physically as well as emotionally. I hurt. The pain in my chest was undeniably strong. My heart was broken—at least, it felt that way. Grief caused me difficulty in sleeping and eating. I had nightmares and my weight dropped from 111 to 98 pounds in six days. Since one's energy reserve is being called upon for overtime, I advise you to get extra rest and to avoid unnecessary fatigue. The body needs energy just to manage daily matters. Do not drink or take drugs, for this effect is only temporary, and sooner or later reality will reappear. At this time one is in a high-tension, high-stress state. Breathing is often fast and shallow, which causes a lack of oxygen to the blood. Sighing is a natural way to relax the body and release stress. It will prevent anxiety, stress, depression, and fatigue.

Crying is essential. It is almost impossible not to release tears after experiencing the death of a loved one. Scientists are presently doing studies to show that the tears of the grieving may contain chemicals that release stress in the body and maintain the body at a comfortable state. So, if talking about your problems leads to tears—let them flow. Crying is a wonderful release.

Adjustment

Grief will hurt whether or not we face it. We can manage to repress it or delay it until it returns in severe physical complaints as mentioned in the stage of shock. Pain is the price we pay for being alive. Ask yourself this question, as I did: "Will the pain I suffer from my loss be productive or will I use it to destroy the rest of my life?"

Adjustment at this point is simply learning to live a life without your loved one. Changes need to be made, but I suggest you do not make any major decisions for at least one year after the death. Think of it as "surviving the seasons." Make plans if you wish, but do not act on them right away. Adjusting to a new life means different things to different people—depending on what the relationship was with the deceased. It takes some time to realize what it is like to live without that special person in your life. This realization usually takes place approximately two to four months after the death. Remember—each new day is a step closer to healing your heart and survival.

Love Will Never Go Away

Spring, and the land lies fresh green
Beneath a yellow sun.
We walked the land together, you and I
And never knew what future days would bring.
Will you often think of me,
When flowers burst forth each year?
When the earth begins to grow again?
Some say death is so final,
But my love for you can never die.
Just as the sun once warmed our hearts,
Let this love touch you some night,
When I am gone,
And loneliness comes—

Before the dawn begins to scatter
Your dreams away.

Summer, and I never knew a bird
Could sing so sweet and clear,
Until they told me I must leave you
For a while.
I never knew the sky could be so deep a blue,
Until I knew I could not grow old with you
But better to be loved by you,
Than to have lived a million summers,
And never knew your love.
Together, let us, you and I

Remember the days and nights,
For eternity.
Fall, and the earth begins to die,
And leaves turn golden-brown upon the trees.
Remember me, too, in autumn, for I will walk with you,
As of old, along a city sidewalk at evening-time,
Though I cannot hold you by the hand.

Winter, and perhaps someday there may be
Another fireplace, another room,
With crackling fire and fragrant smoke,
And turning, suddenly, we will be together,
And I will hear your laughter and touch your face,
And hold you close to me again.
But, until then, if loneliness should seek you out,
Some winter night, when snow is falling down,
Remember, though death has come to me,
Love will never go away!

> Written by Orville Kelly for his wife, Wanda
> (1979, p. 277)

Laughter is definitely the best medicine. You may feel there is no place for laughter during your adjustment to grief or that you will feel guilty if you laugh. But human beings need laughter—your mind and body have limits to the anguish and despair they can withstand. Laughter releases stress and thus alleviates some of the pain.

While we grieve, we need support. I found this support through my friends—the ones who love me no matter what and want to share my hurt. If a friend is not available, bereavement support groups and churches are other means of support.

As time passes, we begin to feel good even if it is just for a brief time. We realize there is hope and we cling to it. At this time we have several tasks to perform in order to continue through the healing process.

1. Letting go—facing the reality of our loved one's death. What has happened cannot be changed. We must accept it. This does not mean forgetting the person. It means being reasonable. Don't make a shrine out of a bedroom or place the deceased on a pedestal, making him or her a saint. Allow your memories to fill you with happiness.
2. Experience the pain—crying and talking about it to those who are willing to listen.
3. Adjusting to the changes—accepting what has happened and learning to live again.
4. Reaching out—reinvesting your emotional energy. Become a volunteer in your community. Contact local organizations or your church to join groups. Sign up for a college course that is appealing to you. The important point is to focus on an interest as a goal. Reach out to others and they will reach out to you.

Your life may never be the same again but it doesn't have to be. If you have hope, then love, peace, and happiness will return. I have always believed one is the master of their own fate. You can make the best out of the worst.

> Blessed are those who mourn for they shall be comforted (Jesus, Sermon on the Mount, Matthew 5:4).

GROWTH

Adjustment leads to growth! You ask, "How can I tell when I've reached this stage?" There is no set time for healing. I believe, from my own experiences, growth begins to take place when one is able to think of the deceased without pain. There will always be a feeling of sadness when you think of the one who has died, but it is a different kind of sadness at this time. You can now think of the deceased without crying. Memories make you smile. You begin to invest your energy into living life again. There will still be "bad days" but they will be less frequent as time passes. The pain never goes completely away. Knowing this and accepting it is half the battle!

The death of your loved one left a gaping hole in your heart and may have opened other wounds from precious losses. Time does heal all wounds, but the scars remain forever. These scars are reminders of our pain, but I also believe they make a positive point. The scars are a part of you and of your struggle through grief. This tragedy is one of your lessons in life. You learn from this experience as you have in the past and as you will in the future. The pain you suffer through grief is one of the most significant factors that shapes you into the person you are. The scars indicate where you've been and what you've done. They are a part of your past and who you are now.

Life is what it is and it is not always fair. Fairness has nothing to do with death. The world cannot be what you want it to be. As you release your unrealistic expectations of life, you make room for self-renewal. You recreate yourself, your goals, your relationships, and your approach to living. Growth takes place when you regain an interest in life and feel more hopeful about your future. It is the time for new beginnings.

Our Growth

Oh, Christ, help us to grow
In our knowledge of you,
In our knowledge of who you would have us be,
In our understanding of what your life means in our lives,
In our understanding of others,
In our comitment to growth in knowledge, understanding,
   love and obedience.

—Avery Brooke (1975, p. 83)

DENIAL

When a death occurs suddenly, the response of close family and friends may be denial. Sometimes this denial is so radical that the survivors do not believe that the person is actually dead—or they know the person is dead, yet not able to believe it. For example, you continue to make plans that include the other person—then reality sets in. Denial may take other forms. A parent will keep a child's room just as it was when he or she died or a widower will continue to say "we" even though only one person is now involved.

There is a desire to avoid the terrible acknowledgment that we have lost what we loved. The world is shaken and the individual is overwhelmed by the impact. As recognition starts to seep in and shock starts to slowly wear off, denial immediately crops up. It is only natural that the bereaved would want or need to deny such a terrible event has happened. At this time the denial is therapeutic. It functions as a buffer by allowing the individual to absorb the reality of the death a little at a time, preventing the survivor from being completely overwhelmed by it. A need to know why the death occurred may appear at this time. Confusion and disorganization are also very common reactions. The initial response might be an intellectualized acceptance of the death, followed by involvement in activities such as funeral arrangements or greeting family and friends. This is an indication that the loss is recognized, but the emotional response to it is denied. If, however, the death itself is denied, then this is an unhealthy response and should receive immediate therapeutic intervention.

Mourning

He is gone; his pain is over and he is gone. The funeral is over and the family and friends have left. The letters are answered. But the emptiness remains. The emptiness and so much. I am angry, God. I am at him for dying and angry at You for letting him die. I am angry at friends who have been so kind, because they are alive and because those they love are alive. I am angry because I failed him so often. I hurt him. I was selfish, thoughtless, mean. And now he is gone, and I cannot undo the past. It might be easier to pretend I am not angry but I cannot fool you, God. Help me through this time of anger and pain, of guilt and loss. Help me to live as he—and You—would like me to live.

— Avery Brooke (1975, p. 84)

ANGER

Anger is a natural part of the healing process after loss. But since anger is a frightening emotion for many of us, we don't like to admit it, let alone permit it. But we should. In fact, we need to. It can be healthy to have anger—even toward a loved one who has died and left us feeling all alone. A widow may be angry at her husband for "deserting" her or a wife angry at her husband for not watching their son more carefully. It's okay to have anger toward the driver of the other car in a tragic accident, or toward God for letting something terrible happen or not answering our prayers. God gets a lot of blame. Anger is the shadow of grief. If we have the courage to use it properly, anger can serve to lift us out of the web of mourning and grief.

It is okay to be sad and it's okay to be mad. You lost someone you love and that makes you angry. It's not right and it's not fair that this person died! Part of our anger is frustration—frustration over the fact that we want to do something to change this reality, but we can't. You're angry because you're not in control. If anger has caught you off guard in your grief, take heart. You can use it to your advantage and gradually heal the pain of loss. Beware, however, feeling angry is sometimes a way to mask our pain. Anger that comes with grief holds the potential to become poisonous. Without proper attention, it will fester and turn into a complete disaster. It can become a nasty habit, a way of life. But, it doesn't have to. The following are a few healthy ways for dealing with anger without delaying grief.

1. Accept and express your feelings
   Allow yourself to be angry but give yourself permission to grieve. If we repress our anger, it will only resurface when we least expect it. One person screams in a private place. Another beats a mattress with a bat. Another does strenuous exercise.
2. Focus on the issues and talk them out.
   Take a moment and consider all the possibilities. Are you angry at a person, a circumstance, yourself, God, or all of them? Discuss them and you will be better able to deal with them. Bottling up anger causes stress, and the cork tends to come off in one way or another, often affecting job performance as well as other relationships.
3. Confront your grief through exercise.
   Exercise is one of the most therapeutic activities. It helps the body release its pent-up desire to lash out in anger. Whether walking, running, biking, or swimming, activity changes the body's biochemistry in positive ways. The workout will help your heart in more ways than one!
4. Get plenty of rest and relaxation.
   To help avoid outbursts of anger, be sure to get enough sleep. Meditation, breathing exercises, and deep muscular relaxation are also good ways to reduce the tension that often occurs before an angry tantrum. Take a course that teaches relaxation methods, or consult your library for books describing these techniques.
5. Apologize to those you became angry with.
   An apology will cleanse your spirit—and it says to the person you lashed out at that you care about the relationship even though you are hurting. Explain your behavior and move on. Remember—you are not alone. No one is exempt from loss, and almost everyone experiences anger because of it. Like other phases of grief, anger may come and go. If you're having trouble communicating your anger in a constructive way or if you're getting angry too often, talk with a friend about your problem and/or see a counselor for help.

I am angry at life for what it has put me through.
I am angry at God, for what he has taken from me.
I am angry at losing what might have been if my brother was alive.
I am angry at friends who weren't there in my family's time of need.
I am angry at myself for the person I am becoming.
I am so full of anger it feels everlasting.
The longer the anger is with me the more of my soul; my sense of
   being is eaten away.
Soon there will be nothing left but an empty shell of anger.

Michael Sten (10/3/97)
(David's brother)

Denial, anger and depression are often regarded as unhealthy responses to death. But an important distinction needs to be made between reactions which are part of a naturally evolving process of self-protection and those which are potentially harmful, both for oneself and others (Reoch, 1996, p. 112).

GUILT

As if all these other feelings aren't enough, you feel guilty, too. Some guilt is appropriate and some isn't. You need to deal with it for what it is. Sometimes you are guilty. You need to be able to face that and accept it. Sometimes we need to seek forgiveness, especially from ourselves.

Few survivors escape the grief process without some feeling of guilt. You may feel guilty because you did not make sure your loved one took care of her health or got to the doctor sooner. A sudden or accidental death may give rise to the torture of all kinds of "if only's."

Whatever your situation, realize that feelings of guilt and regret are normal. There is a difference between normal guilt and neurotic guilt. Normal guilt is the guilt we feel when we have done something or neglected to do something for which we ought to feel guilty. Neurotic guilt is feeling guilty out of proportion to our own real involvement in a particular situation. A good example of normal guilt would be the guilt we have when we lose a loved one through death. It would be impossible to not feel guilty about some of the things we did not do for this person when he or she was alive, or the things we did do that hurt this person when he or she was with us. We know we have made mistakes in thought, word, and deed and we should feel guilty about it. This is normal. It happens to everyone at some time in their life. If you made mistakes in your relationship with your loved one, do not dwell on them. Focus on the positive times.

An example of neurotic guilt might be a daughter who has stayed by her aged father's bedside in the hospital for days without sleep. The doctor suggests that she go home and get some sleep. She leaves and her father dies. She will never forgive herself for not being there when it happened. She dwells on it endlessly and builds it up out of proportion to the real situation. Unresolved guilt and misunderstood emotions of this type can make us miserable for years. It is important for us to confront our guilt and dispose of it. Accept your fallibility. Get professional help if necessary.

> Love is an endless act of forgiveness.
> — Author Unknown

ANXIETY

Anxiety is feeling afraid even in familiar situations. Sometimes we feel "panic." This might be a general feeling of fear or it could be worse—an acute anxiety reaction. You're terrified and don't know of what! You feel nervous. You feel afraid—afraid to be alone and afraid to be with other people; afraid to stay home and afraid to go out—afraid of everything. It is a terrible experience, especially when it happens for the first time. You really wonder if you're going crazy because you seem to have no control over your own panic! You think that other people don't feel this way and there's something wrong with you. But, other people do have these feelings.

When you panic, you feel jumpy and nervous. You might feel as if your whole body is trembling. You might have a nervous stomach and feel as if you're going to be sick. Your whole body feels uncomfortable, and you are short of breath. You just can't seem to get enough air. It's as if you're suffocating. You can't concentrate. Your thoughts and feelings are everywhere. You can't think of anything except of the person who died. Sound familiar? It is familiar to a lot of people.

The feeling of loss of control is present in grief. We didn't have control over the person's death and now we seem to have little control over our own reactions. There is a real connection between these two events. Most of us experience self-control in our lives. We choose what we do and make the most of our own decisions. Now, death has suddenly intervened and we have no control. We can't do anything about it. It's overwhelming—more than we can bear.

We need to reassure ourselves that we do have some control over our lives. By simply trying to accept the feeling of anxiety and recognize that it's a normal part of grieving, it will lessen more and more each day. When you fight the anxiety, you're feeding it energy. One way to combat it is to replace it with something, such as a pleasant memory of your loved one.

BETRAYAL

The American Heritage Dictionary defines "betrayal" as the act of:

- giving aid or information to an enemy
- committing treason against or to be a traitor
- being disloyal or unfaithful
- divulging in a breach of confidence
- deceiving or leading astray

It's funny how some people, within months of Leo's death, were trying to set me up with men. They would go out of their way to introduce me to single men at parties, and then when I met someone on my own, I heard comments like "Don't you think it might be too soon for you to date?" When Paul and I set a date to be married (two years later!), people were shocked and said, "Well, it didn't take you long to find someone new." How can people be so cruel? Human beings need one another. According to the above definitions, I certainly wasn't betraying Leo. Besides, those ties were broken when he died. Isn't that what the wedding vows mean—"until death do we part?" My father-in-law became involved with another woman a few months after the death of my mother-in-law after thirty-five years of marriage. That doesn't mean he loved his wife any less—it's just human nature.

Miss Me–But Let Me Go

When I come to the end of the road
And the sun has set for me,
I want no rites in a gloom filled room
Why cry for a soul set free.

Miss me a little—but not too long
And not with your head bowed low,
Remember the love that we once shared
Miss me—but let me go.

For this is a journey that we all must take
And each must go alone,
It's all a part of the Maker's plan
A step on the road to home.

When you are lonely and sick of heart
Go to the friends we know,
And bury your sorrows in doing good deeds
Miss me—but let me go.

— Author Unknown

This is time for the removal of all barriers. The barriers between ourselves and others, the barriers between our own mind and the inner depths of our being. The barriers which create anxiety and tension, mistrust and uncertainty, divisiveness and resentment (Reoch, 1996, p. 142).

UNFINISHED BUSINESS

Each moment we all face the possibility that we will not be alive the next moment to complete a particular task, but the possibility that we will not be alive is so small that we simultaneously ignore it and deny it. Unfinished business refers to those issues that were never addressed or lacked successful closure in the relationship. Besides referring to practical matters such as planning a will or tying up loose ends in business, the term also focuses on psychosocial issues between the survivor and the deceased. Concerns such as:

- Were they able to talk about what they needed or wanted to express to one another?
- Could they explain to one another why they were upset about a particular situation?
- Were they able to express their regrets?
- Did they get to say thank you or I'm sorry?
- Were they able to express their love for one another?
- Did they get to say good-bye to each other?

Unfinished business is just that—unfinished! This lack of closure may cause intense anxiety. Some grievers may feel they cannot relinquish their grief until they find an end to that which was unfinished—so they fail to grieve. Following the unexpected loss of a loved one, you may have a need to bring closure to your relationship with that person. Thoughts and feelings you never fully shared with the deceased fill you with a sense of incompleteness. You search for a way to say the unsaid "I love you" or "I'm sorry." If this sense of incompleteness continues, you need to address your unfulfilled relationship. In order to express your thoughts and feelings, you might try writing letters to the person who has died (as I did to Leo), keeping a personal journal, or speaking directly to your deceased loved one. Such activities can help you to resolve the unexpressed feelings that can be so pronounced following a sudden death. The less unfinished business between the survivor and the deceased means less emotional baggage for the griever to cope with after the death.

ANNIVERSARY DATES

Certain days or times of the year that have significance (for example, birthdays, date of death, holidays, seasons, wedding days, etc.) can trigger thoughts of the deceased, and some of the earlier pain may return for a short period of time. This reaction is an increase in the intensity of the grief response at certain times even after there has been some resolution to the death of a loved one. As long as this response subsides after the anniversary period passes—even if it occurs year after year—it is a necessary step toward the healing process. If, however, an old wound is opened and the pain shows no evidence of ending, aspects of unresolved grief may still exist and professional assistance may be required.

While most of us, during our grief process, cannot remember a number, a name, or a face for more than a few minutes, our heads are loaded with significant dates we cannot seem to forget. You know how long it's been since the death down to the hour. As we work our way through the grief process, we dispense with the hourly count; however, these dates remain on our mind's calendar.

Difficult as it is to imagine, those anniversary dates that cause us so much apprehension and anxiety do fade with the years. There is no reason to feel disloyal when a special date passes quietly unnoticed until days later. Acknowledge the day. Celebrate if you wish. The memories are part of your life. Don't dismiss them!

FRIENDSHIP

Most people view grief as a negative experience, but if we can see it as a process one goes through to regain health and increase personal growth, then it can be a positive experience. The length of the grief process depends mostly on the survivor's willingness to do his or her grief work. From my own experience, I know that one cannot separate oneself from grief—not for long anyway. And while you do, a part of you dies with it. You, the survivor, need time to deal with it. Unfortunately, one cannot grieve alone. Grief requires a relationship with another human being—someone who is willing to listen to you over and over again—a friend.

If it had not been for my friends, I would not have grown to be the healthy person I am today. I needed them and they were there to console me, comfort me, and do what they could to help. I needed them to listen to me. They heard the same story a hundred times! Talk about your loved one—it's a good therapeutic way to release tension.

Eventually the visits stop and the telephone does not ring quite as often. This lack of attention was mainly due to people being busy with their own lives. They have good intentions when they assume that you will be able to function once again. The sad part is they are often unaware of how long the grieving process is unless they have been there. Do not blame them for what appears to be a lack of concern, for they have no clue of how lonely you may feel.

When visiting your "couple friends" after the death of a spouse, you will begin to feel like a third wheel and eventually many of these friends will drift away. You are no longer a twosome. You are single and available. Wives or husbands whose marriages are hanging on by a thread may now consider you a threat. Unfortunately, many friendships fade where couples are involved.

It is very important for you to get involved in several activities in order to develop new relationships with both men and women. Many of your friends will feel it is necessary to match you up so they will invite single men to a gathering that you will be present for. Get out and meet people—the rest will fall in place!

I have included here a list of things you can do, as a friend, for someone who has experienced the death of a loved one.

1. Accept her emptiness or tears with equal compassion, knowing that both exist because of pain.
2. Show empathy. Walk in her shoes and try to experience what she is really feeling. This may be difficult if you have never experienced the death of someone close to you. If this is the case, just listen. How important this is!
3. Open your heart with love—not judgment. When I was grieving, I craved that love!
4. Don't stay away. Stay with your friend and hurt with her. She needs your comforting—your presence. She needs to know that you are there for her. Your visits need not be lengthy unless the bereaved specifically requests otherwise. Just stopping by will let your friend know you care. But remember, her privacy is important, too.
5. Run errands. Offer to drive your friend to the doctor or even do some shopping for her. Insist and be firm. Let her know you really want to.
6. Bring a gift—a book, candy, perfume, or a single rose. These unexpected gifts will show your love and support for a longer period of time.
7. Your bereaved friend will always remember dates of the events associated with her loved one's death. When others remember,

the day is brighter. Call or send a card to acknowledge the event. This has greater meaning than you will ever know. Remember the forgotten mourners as well—children, siblings, grandparents, or other friends—anyone who was especially close.

8. Be patient. Sometimes the bereaved will push close friends away because the memories are unbearable. This is what generally causes many friendships to fade away. This rejection places a strain on both parties. Understanding what is going on inside your friend is crucial. Close friends remind the bereaved of "the way it used to be." This can be so painful. It takes time to confront such realities. It is important to maintain contact but understand refused invitations.

9. Allow the grieving person to talk about the deceased and listen—really listen.

10. Give your friend permission to grieve. Let her know it's all right to feel the way she does.

11. Remember that nothing you say will stop the grieving person's pain. Just be there!

12. Most important, be yourself. Your grieving friend will know and appreciate this later. It is the one thing I truly remember— who my real friends were!

It is a challenge to love the bereaved. You see pain, and possibly feel it, but cannot remove it. You are asked to give love without receiving anything in return. It is an opportunity for you to learn about yourself—to see the truth in your own heart and to grow from it. In summary, love your friend as she grieves, listen to her, be patient, accept her as she is, and have hope.

As a friend to someone who has experienced the death of a loved one, here are some things you really should not do!

1. Don't say, "I know how you feel." Remember, each person's grief is unique and no one can totally understand another's grief even if you have been there before.

2. Don't be afraid of your own tears. A friend will remember who cries with them.

3. Don't avoid the grieving person because you don't know what to say. Say nothing—just hug them or offer your hand to hold.

4. Don't say, "I'm here for you" and then not be there!

5. Don't say, "Be strong" or "Don't cry." The grieving person may begin to repress her feelings.

6. Don't say, "Its God's will" or "He's at rest now."

7. Don't make statements that induce guilt or blame. Unfinished business causes enough guilt.

8. Don't change the subject when the bereaved talks about her loved one. Listen!

9. Don't try to answer the question, "Why?" Take their hand and squeeze it. Just comfort them.

10. Don't say, "You're young; you'll get married again" or "At least you have other children."

11. Don't encourage the grieving person to "get over it." This is only a sign of your own discomfort.

> There is a way of listening which is a way of giving, and another way of listening which is a way of refusing, of refusing oneself . . . the person who is at my disposal is the one who is capable of being with me with the whole of himself when I am in need; while the one who is not at my disposal seems merely to offer me a temporary loan raised on his resources. For the one I am a presence; for the other I am an object. Presence involves a reciprocity . . . (Marcel, 1962, p. 40).

HUGS

To press tightly, especially in the arms, is Webster's definition of a hug. Skin-hunger, some call it. The skin is the largest organ of the human body—the sensor of temperature, judge of texture, instrument of emotional contact. The skin is the prison within which we live, the barrier which isolates us from one another—until we reach across and touch another person.

It's no small thing—this need for a hug. Most of us need physical affection, as reassurance that we are lovable and loved. This is more so in times of personal crisis—when emotional suffering makes us doubt our own and others' goodness. The best remedy for melting away our pain is a warm embrace.

Popular psychology insists that we all need hugs every day, several times a day. It is my personal belief that we need at least five good hugs to get us through the day. And if we are going through a difficult time in our lives, all the more reason to seek and to give even more hugs!

There are plenty of good huggers around. Leo Buscaglia, the "love doctor" who wrote about the importance of love and physical affection, was one of the best. You probably know someone like Leo Buscaglia—a family member, a friend, a neighbor, a co-worker, or a member of your congregation or club. Think of all the huggers you know and every time you see them, ask for a hug! Nothing will please these warmhearted, compassionate people more than to be asked for a hug. It's their mission in life!

If you find it difficult to locate someone willing to respond to your need for a hug, then search for someone who needs a hug. Visit a hospital, a nursing home, a retirement or day-care program, or an orphanage. It may take longer and a little more effort to satisfy your skin hunger, but the reward is well worth it—the joy of bringing a smile to someone else's face.

If nothing seems to work or you just can't reach out to touch someone, don't give up. It doesn't mean you're unloving or an unlovable person. You just have to learn to loosen the cap a little so that affection you have all bottled up inside of you can seep out! Practice makes perfect!

A Hug

There's something in a simple hug
That always warms the heart.
It welcomes us back home
And makes it easier to part.
A hug's a way to share the joy
And sad times we go through.
Or just a way for friends to say
They like you 'cause you're you.
Hugs are meant for anyone
For whom we really care.
From your grandma to your neighbor,
Or a cuddly teddy bear.
A hug is an amazing thing.
It's just the perfect way
To show the love we're feeling
But can't find the words to say.
It's funny how a little hug
Makes everyone feel good.
In every place and language
It's always understood.
And hugs don't need new equipment,
Special batteries or parts.
Just open up your arms and open up your hearts.

— Author Unknown

Hugging

Hugging is healthy; it helps the body's immune system. It keeps you healthier, it helps cure depression, reduce stress, induce sleep. It's invigorating; it's rejuvenating. It has no unpleasant side effects, and it is nothing short of a miracle drug.

Hugging is all natural; it's organic; it's naturally sweet, with no pesticides, no preservatives, no artificial ingredients, and it's 100 percent wholesome.

Hugging is practically perfect. There are no movable parts, no batteries to wear out, no periodic checkups. It is low energy consumption, high energy yield, inflation proof, non-fattening, has no monthly payments and no insurance requirements. It is theft proof, non-taxable, non-polluting and, of course, it's fully returnable!

— Author Unknown
Contributed by Kay Bensen
East Meadow Alzheimer's Support Group
Long Island Alzheimer's Foundation

HANDLING THE HOLIDAYS

Getting through the holidays and those special dates was extremely difficult. It was like reliving the death all over again. The tears come and sadness lingers awhile. Each event is dealt with for the first time. The worst, however, seems to be the anniversary of the death itself. Leo died the day after Mother's Day and each year the wound opens again.

Others have shared with me a variety of ways in which they were able to deal with these difficult days; I share them with you.

1. First and foremost, take care of yourself. Grief is exhausting. You don't sleep and the constant crying is draining. In the beginning I didn't care what I looked like or if I ate. In fact, I didn't care about anything—not even my daughter. As time passes, you begin to feel better. The following is a list of things you must do for yourself.
   - Eat well-balanced meals
   - Get dressed in the morning
   - Plan a morning and evening activity
   - Have dinner with someone two or three nights a week
   - Exercise regularly
   - Pamper yourself
2. Take a walk along the beach or go for a drive for peace and quiet.
3. Get involved in a project to honor your loved one, such as painting a picture or making a collage of photos and memories.

4. Begin a quilt by sewing a square together on each special event. Continue this on days when you are feeling especially sad. The quilt can serve as a memorial for your loved one.

5. Plant a garden with the favorite flowers and vegetables of the deceased. This therapeutic activity releases stress and lifts your spirits. It brings one closer to nature and reassures us that life goes on.

6. Adopt a pet. They are a wonderful source of comfort because they give love unconditionally and don't mind when their owners are cranky and feeling down. The warmth they provide and the dedication they show means a lot to people who are feeling barely alive.

> Do not stand at my grave and weep.
> I am not there, I do not sleep.
> I am a thousand winds that blow;
> I am the diamond glints on snow.
> I am the sunlight on ripened grain,
> I am the gentle autumn rain.
> When you awake in the morning hush,
> I am the swift, uplifting rush
> Of quiet birds in circling flight.
> I am the soft starlight at night.
> Do not stand at my grave and weep. I am not there.
> I do not sleep.
>
> — Makahindian Prayer

Roses For Rose

Red roses were her favorites, her name was also Rose.
And every year her husband sent them, tied with pretty bows.
The year he died, the roses were delivered to her door.
The card said, "Be My Valentine," like all the years before.

Each year he sent her roses, and the note would always say,
"I love you even more this year, than last year on this day."
"My love for you will always grow, with every passing year."
She knew this was the last time that the roses would appear.

She thought, he ordered roses in advance before this day.
Her loving husband did not know, that he would pass away.
He always liked to do things early, way before the time.
Then, if he got too busy, everything would work out fine.

She trimmed the stems, and placed them in a very special vase.
Then, sat the vase beside the portrait of his smiling face.
She would sit for hours, in her husband's favorite chair.
While staring at his picture, and the roses sitting there.

A year went by, and it was hard to live without her mate.
With loneliness and solitude, that had become her fate.
Then, the very hour, as on Valentines before,
The doorbell rang, and there were roses, sitting by her door.

She brought the roses in, and then just looked at them in shock.
Then, went to get the telephone, to call the florist shop.
The owner answered, and she asked him, if he would explain,
Why would someone do this to her, causing her so much pain?

"I know your husband passed away, more than a year ago,"
The owner said, "I knew you'd call, and you would want to
    know."
"The flowers you received today, were paid for in advance."
"Your husband always planned ahead, he left nothing to chance."

"There is a standing order, that I have on file down here,
And he has paid, well in advance, you'll get them every year.
There also is another thing, that I think you should know,
He wrote a special little card . . . he did this years ago."

"Then, should ever, I find out that he's no longer here,
That's the card . . . that should be sent, to you the following year."
She thanked him and hung up the phone, her tears now flowing
    hard.
Her fingers shaking, as she slowly reached to get the card.

Inside the card, she saw that he had written her a note.
Then, as she stared in total silence, this is what he wrote . . .
"Hello, my love, I know it's been a year since I've been gone,
I hope it hasn't been too hard for you to overcome."

"I know it must be lonely, and the pain is very real.
For if it was the other way, I know how I would feel.
The love we shared made everything so beautiful in life.
I loved you more than words can say, you were the perfect wife."

"You were my friend and lover, you fulfilled my every need.
I know it's only been a year, but please try not to grieve.
I want you to be happy, even when you shed your tears.
That is why the roses will be sent to you for years."

"When you get these roses, think of all the happiness,
That we had together, and how both of us were blessed.
I have always loved you and I know I always will.
But, my love, you must go on, you have some living still."

"Please . . . try to find happiness, while living out your days.
I know it is not easy, but I hope you find some ways.
The roses will come every year, and they will only stop,
When your door's not answered, when the florist stops to knock."

"He will come five times that day, in case you have gone out.
But after his last visit, he will know without a doubt,
To take the roses to the place, where I've instructed him,
And place the roses where we are, together once again."

— Author Unknown

I'm Here!

The Rogers are devout Christians who have built a strong family.
The father has a special interest in the spiritual condition of each of
his children and often would quiz them in order to know if they
were sure of their salvation. Occasionally he would ask them to
share in their own words about their relationship with Jesus
Christ.

One day it was seven-year-old Jimmy's turn to express how he
knew he had eternal life. Jimmy hold his version: "I think it will be
something like this in Heaven. One day when we all get to go to
Heaven, it will be time for the big angel to read from the big book
the names of all the people who will be there. He will come to the
Rogers family and say, 'Daddy Rogers?' And Daddy will say, 'Here!"
Then the angel will call out, 'Mommy Rogers?' and Mommy will say
'Here!' Then the angel will come down to call out Susie Rogers and
Mavis Rogers, and they will both say, 'Here!' "

He paused, took a big deep breath and continued. "And finally
that big angel will read my name, Jimmy Rogers, and because I'm
little and maybe he'll miss me, I'll jump and shout really loud,
'Here!' to make sure he knows I'm there."

Just a few days later there was a tragic accident. A car struck
down little Jimmy Rogers as he made his way to catch the school
bus. He was rushed by ambulance to the hospital, and all the family
was summoned. He was in critical condition.

The little family group gathered around the bed in which little
Jimmy now lay with no movement, no consciousness, and no hope
for recovery. The doctors had done all that was in their power.
Jimmy would probably be gone by morning.

The family prayed and waited. Late in the night the little boy
seemed to be stirring a bit. They all moved closer. They saw his lips
move; just one word was all he uttered before he passed from this

life. But what a word of comfort and hope for a grieving family he was to leave behind. In the clear voice of a little boy, loud and clear enough so all could hear and understand, little Jimmy Rogers said the one word: "Here!" And then he was gone to another life beyond this world, where a big angel was reading the names of all those written there.

— Robert Strand (1996)
Excerpted from *Moments for Mothers*

COMMUNITY SERVICE

About a year after Leo died, I decided to do some volunteer work. I went from hospital to nursing home and back again, but just couldn't seem to find my niche. I finally gave up and decided it was because I just wasn't ready to do it. After I went back to school in 1989, I decided to try again. Since I was doing my nurse's aid training in a local nursing home, I thought it would be nice to do my volunteer work in a hospital. After buying my uniform and putting in two weeks of volunteer work, I quit. I don't normally leave anything undone so I was pretty upset with myself. Something just didn't seem right with me when it came to volunteer work. Another year went by and I tried again—at the hospital where Leo died. Again, it didn't work, but I realized it was because of the hospital environment. I had spent so much time in the Intensive Care Unit while Leo was in his coma that I suppose subconsciously everything came back to me when I tried to volunteer.

While I was at the hospital, I saw a sign that read Hospice and inquired about it—mostly out of curiosity. Ironically, the following semester I took a course called Death and Dying, taught by Mary Jane Ringkamp, the person to whom this book is dedicated. She introduced herself to the class and mentioned her affiliation with Hospice of the South Shore. She explained Hospice to us and I realized then that was where I wanted to be.

In 1993, I called Hospice and requested an application for volunteer training. I graduated from the program in May of 1994. Hospice volunteers are specially prepared through a twenty-four-hour comprehensive education program. They serve as a good friend to the patient and family. Volunteers also assist Hospice by working in a variety of other services; such as fund raising and public relations.

Hospice (for those of you who are not familiar with it) is a philosophy—not a facility—one that emphasizes and affirms life. Hospice is palliative care for the dying; it accentuates the quality of life, as defined by the patient, when quantity of life is limited. The purpose of Hospice is to enable individuals with a terminal illness to be cared for at home so they can live out their final days in comfort and peace among their loved ones in familiar settings. The Hospice approach provides a comprehensive medical model that addresses the psychological, social, and spiritual dimensions of care, as well as the physical, when cure is no longer a reasonable expectation. It includes the patient's family and loved ones and pays particular attention to their needs, supporting the family's traditional strengths and coping skills in the face of crisis.

Hospice, of course, is not the only area one can serve as a volunteer, but the people involved with this concept are warm and compassionate human beings. They gave me an outlet to serve others. They are very special people in my heart.

Other areas in which you may offer your volunteer services are:

- nursing homes and special care facilities
- hospitals
- rehabilitation centers for the disabled
- day nurseries
- emergency shelters for the homeless
- summer camps
- maternity homes and child placement services

The Troubles of Others

God, help us to enter into the troubles of others, know them as if they were our own and act accordingly.
— Avery Brooke, 1975, p. 71

SPIRITUAL GROWTH

A religious upbringing that emphasized sin and its punishments more than God's loving compassion can intensify the guilt one feels. You may want to seek out a pastoral counselor or spiritual director to help you distinguish between authentic religious guilt (adult awareness of a specific wrong committed and its implications for your relationship with God) and psychological guilt (the shame of feeling not good enough). This kind of spiritual direction may help you to feel reconciled once again with a God who has never stopped loving you, whatever you may have done or not done in the relationship with your deceased loved one. Many people find that some form of confession—either sacramental or to a trusted friend—relieves the burden of guilt and helps them to feel God's forgiveness.

In your need to find a meaning related to your loss you may feel anger at God, and a need to question "Why did this happen?" You may question, temporarily abandon, or change your belief system, or you may become more religious than in the past or search for answers or meaning in death—and even life. These feelings and responses may come in waves of greater or lesser intensity and are normal experiences of grief.

Spiritual growth is one of the rewards we find when we pursue our journey through grief. When the remains of our turmoil are sorted through and cleared away, we uncover the path leading to our spiritual growth.

Some individuals regard life on earth as a lower or less adequate form of life than existence after death. Life on earth requires struggles, pain, disturbances, stress, decay; life after death is filled with peace, love, happiness, fulfillment, and a sense of harmony. Leading a spiritual life brings one to this kind of immorality, which signifies that one is "in harmony with a principle extending beyond the limited biological life span" (Lifton, 1977, p. 278). One example of spiritual immortality is "nirvana"—a state that is undefinable, immeasurable, and infinite and not a state of annihilation (Watts, 1957). In nirvana one is released from the pains of going through continuous lives. The issue of consciousness seems to be resolved by the definite assumption that self-consciousness ceases when nirvana is achieved.

The Western counterpart to the Buddhist nirvana is often expressed as "being at one" with God, nature, the universe, or with humanity. It is not clearly defined because it disregards definition. The belief generally includes cancellation of the meaning of time as well as of the meaning of matter. That is, all time is now; all matter is matter and is unity or one single whole—and psychological life ceases. If these ideas strike you as strange or even ridiculous, you are not alone! If you can grasp what the words mean or if something in you is attuned to their meaning—again you are not alone!

Gibran says, "Yesterday we crawled in fright like shuddering ghosts between the fears of the night and the menaces of the day." Yesterday our fears, our grief, our anxiety, and our anger disconnected us from our spiritual self—but only temporarily.

Spirituality is an internal gauge we can use to measure the external world. It unites body, mind, and spirit and makes us whole once again. A healthy person nurtures the spirit as well as the body and mind. These three components must be harmonious before we can experience intense moments of clarity and awareness. We feel whole and at one with ourselves and our spirits.

Our inner spirits are known by many different names—Higher Power, Allah, Buddha, Jehovah, Life Energy, Cosmic Power, etc. Whatever one chooses to refer to it as, it is a constant source of strength and energy that guides us when we experience a loss. We realize that we are not going through this alone—that a part of ourselves connects us to a higher consciousness and helps us gain a sense of direction and more positive values. When we accept the existence of our spiritual self, we gain a sense of direction and more positive values.

Each day of our recovery is like receiving a gift. We become stronger, better, and more productive in what we set out to do. Everything takes on a new light and becomes important to us again. Build on your memories. Though you must accept your loved one's death, you need not sever all ties. You can use memories to establish a new kind of relationship, and you can find ways for those memories to enrich your life. Recall the humorous times and laugh about them. Some will disapprove if you laugh "too soon," but it's not disrespectful. Remembering with laughter is therapeutic.

Many survivors become involved in their loved one's work or interest. Find an organization through which you can assist other bereaved people. Realize that you may be at a place in your life where new opportunities for service or involvement should be explored. This may be the time to return to school, become active in church, or volunteer at a health facility. Whatever you do, do not waste your life in unproductive sorrow. The best memorial to a loved one is a full and growing life.

In our dark moments we may not have an answer to the riddle of suffering. But we can surrender ourselves into the hands of One who does have the answers and who will faithfully walk us through the dark valley of grief. Prayer and meditation can be excellent paths to inner peace and balance. If you are feeling too distressed to pray or sit quietly, don't forget that there is a host of excellent spiritual books and tapes. Another choice would be to write two or three pages a day in a journal. You can use this time to carry on a conversation with God or simply to let out some of the feelings that may be welling up inside. There is great value in expressing your pain, getting it out in the open, on a page, in a drawing—whatever mode of expression best suits you. Consider each and every one of these efforts to be a healing—because they are. It isn't easy to be thankful and sad at the same time. Try to spend a little time thinking of the many things in your life for which you are grateful. With time, you will begin to feel gratitude for the painful lessons you are learning as you move through your grief.

Spiritual growth is an ongoing process. By giving attention to our spiritual needs, we become stronger in our daily lives. All things pass— including the overwhelming pain that you may be feeling right now. It is only human to cry out for relief. Surely it will soon come from the God who loved you first.

> We are laid asleep
> In body, and become a living soul:
> While with an eye made quiet by the power
> Of harmony, and the deep power of joy,
> We see into the life of things.
> — William Wordsworth

JOURNAL WRITING

Many times there will be no one around with whom to share and, even if there is, you may not feel like talking. Writing down your feelings can be extremely helpful. You need to keep in touch with whom you are throughout this loss, and more so who you are becoming. You want to keep in touch with the feelings that accompany the movement of your life from death to a new life. Through writing, we become more conscious of our inner thoughts, emotional responses, and experiences. When we put words into a concrete, written form, we capture the essence of a life and experience the miracles of self-discovery through self-expression.

Keeping a journal is not the same as keeping a diary. You are not writing what happened during the day, but how you are feeling and why you are feeling that way. You need to be in contact with the ups and downs of your life, so that the direction and the flow of your life become more evident. Try to record significant events of the day and how you felt about each. On some days you may write a full page and on other days only a few lines. You may not record something every day. The goal is to get down on paper what is inside of you. And do not write just when you are down; the good days are just as important! Over weeks and months you will be able to gauge your progress. You will be able to view the change in your emotional patterns. Writing helps you to reflect on your words as they are put on paper. It gives form and expression to the feelings inside you. You will find yourself expressing feelings you were not even aware you had. Writing helps you see inside yourself!

HOPE

According to *The American Heritage Dictionary*, "hope" is defined as:

- to obtain a wish for something with some expectation

- to be confident; trust
- to look forward with confidence of its fulfillment
- that which is desired or anticipated

Throughout this book I have mentioned the word "hope" at least twenty times. The above definitions do not totally satisfy my feeling for what hope really means. To me, hope is having faith that my world is basically a very nice place and can even get better. By having this thing called "hope" I can risk letting go of some of my problems and trusting that something good will happen to take care of things.

Fyodor Dostoyevsky, the great novelist, said not to lose hope nor give up, no matter how hard things may be, for this is the purpose of life. He believed that human goodness and strength came not from success, but from suffering. My hope then, throughout my grief, was that in the end I would become a stronger person through all my suffering. I saw how others rose above their problems. I listened to situations that were worse than my own. I absorbed the atmosphere of love and goodwill. That gave me a new lease on life. It gave me hope.

> After all, hope contains no mono or polyunsaturated fats, cholesterol, sugars, artificial sweeteners, flavors or colors; it's classified as "generally recognized as safe" by the FDA and is a known anticarcinogen (Munson, 1993, p. 24).

Tomorrow Is Not Promised

Sometimes people come into your life
and you know right away that they were meant to be there,
they serve some sort of purpose,
teach you a lesson
or help figure out who you are
and who you want to become.

You never know who these people may be:
your neighbor, child, long lost friend, lover, or even a complete stranger
who, when you lock eyes with them,
you know at that very moment that they will affect your life
in some profound way.

And sometimes things happen to you
and at the time they seem painful and unfair,
but in reflection you realize
that without overcoming those obstacles
you would have never realized
your potential strength, will power, or heart.

Everything happens for a reason.
Nothing happens by chance
or by means of good or bad luck.
Illness, injury, love, lost moments of true greatness and sheer stupidity
all occur to test the limits of your soul.

Without these small tests,
whether they be events, illnesses or relationships,
life would be like a smoothly paved straight flat road to nowhere,
safe and comfortable,
but dull and utterly pointless.

The people you meet who affect your life
and the successes and downfalls you experience
create who you are,
and even the bad experiences can be learned from,
In fact, they are probably the poignant and important ones.

If someone hurts you, betrays you or greaks your heart,
forgive them,
for they have helped you learn about trust
and the importance of being cautious to
whom you open your heart . . .

If someone loves you,
love them back unconditionally,
not only because they love you,
but because they are teaching you to love
and opening your heart and eyes to things
you would have never seen or felt without them.

Make every day count.
Appreciate every moment
and take from it everything that you possibly can,
for you may never be able to experience it again . . .

Talk to people you have never talked to before,
and actually listen,
let yourself fall in love,
break free and set your sights high . . .

Hold your head up
because you have every right to.
Tell yourself you are a great individual and believe in yourself . . .
for if you don't believe in yourself,
no one else will believe in you either.
You can make of your life anything you wish.

Create your own life
and then go out and live in it!
"Live Each Day As If It Were Your Last . . .
Tomorrow is Not Promised"

— Author Unknown

God, Is This Just One More Mountain to Climb?

God, is this just one more mountain to climb?
Or is it my last?
I must confess, it looks so high . . .
Not sure if I can climb this one, this time
I'm really afraid
but that is just between you and me,
I wouldn't say that to anyone else.
I feel tears in my eyes, tears in my heart.
Looking back I've had so much.
I am thankful.
Never fully appreciating . . .
God, is this just one more mountain to climb?
Or is it my last?
Are you going to give me the strength and courage
I need to reach the top this time?
I've lived, I've cried
I've laughed, I've loved
but I feel like I have so much more
that I want to do in my life.
God, is this just one more mountain to climb?
Or is it my last?
Please, I want so much to reach the peak again.
I want to float on my own special cloud again.
I've so much more laughter, so much more passion
for life.
So much more love to give.
Please, God, the tears are beginning to well up in me now.
Is this just one more mountain to climb?
Or is it my last?

— Sue Bell 202
Copyright August 8, 1998

PART THREE

Death Awareness

CHAPTER 3

Being Prepared

I cannot stress enough how important it is to be prepared for the death of family members as well as for your own. We plan for every aspect of life—from having a family, vacations, weddings, and retirement. We also prepare for what might happen if a fire or accident occurs. But, what about death? Most of us do not like to think about death— especially our own. We avoid making important funeral decisions in advance. It is very important to plan ahead because dealing with the state or government agencies can be very frustrating.

Having to deal with making funeral arrangements immediately following a death is confusing and upsetting for many family members. Often they do not have the information needed to claim benefits. Planning ahead prevents emotional overspending and protects your family's interests. It helps give meaning to a person's life. It enables family and friends to come together to express feelings of grief and sadness. It helps family and friends accept the reality of death, so they can overcome the emotional pain. By planning now, you can relieve stress and take away part of the burden on family and friends later.

What to do with disposition of the body is one of the most basic decisions in funeral planning. Earth burial is the most common method of disposition. The body is placed in a casket, and set in a grave. Burial occurs after a service or ceremony, or without any service. It requires buying a cemetery plot, a grave liner or vault (if required), and a grave marker or monument. Entombment is when the body is placed in a casket and laid to rest in an above-ground tomb, or mausoleum. Cremation is a heat process which reduces the remains to ashes and particles of bone. The cremated remains can be buried, stored in a vault, kept at home in an urn, or scattered on private property or, perhaps, out at sea. It might be a good idea to ask the funeral director about any legal restrictions. A funeral ceremony or memorial service can still take place with or without the body or remains present. A simple disposition is taking the body directly to a cemetery or crematory. Embalming, viewing of the body, and casket may not be required. A memorial service or remembrance service may take place afterward.

Choose a funeral director that you like and trust, talk over the options, and make your choices. Pay cash if you can and read the fine print carefully to make sure that what you want is paid for and that no additional charges can be added—no matter how many years may pass before you take delivery of the services.

With your funeral arrangements made, sit down and write out some instructions about what you would like to happen at your funeral or memorial service. Make your wishes known. Keep it handy (not in a safe deposit box where it may be difficult to get at). Let your family or close friends know where your plan is, or give them a copy.

One is never too young to have a will written. Hire a lawyer and decide how your property should be divided. Leo was only thirty-one and we had not been married long enough to think of a will. Our neighbor was discussing his plans for when he died and Leo laughed and said, "I'm not going to die for a long time."

Two weeks later he was dead. Dying "intestate"—not having a will—caused me a lot of legal problems because our automobiles were still in separate names! This means the estate, including property and assets belonging to the deceased, will be disbursed according to state law. This will not include property where the title is in the name of the deceased and another person. This property will automatically pass on to the co-owner. There are a lot of paperwork and hassles to deal with. I won, but only after several months and many unnecessary headaches.

Besides having a will to direct the disposal of your property, one should have a "Living Will." This recent development is an attempt to prevent unusual means from being used to keep you alive. The purpose of this concept is to allow you to exert control over how you will be medically treated should you be diagnosed with an incurable disease or other terminal incident. A sample of a "living will" is shown on p. 113.

It is important to note that a living will is not always enough. Medical experts can, in some cases, dispute, disregard, or postpone the desires expressed in a living will. They cannot, however, argue with a document called a Durable Power of Attorney for Healthcare. Specific rules vary from state to state. It can be as easy as putting a few simple words on plain paper. In discussion of Powers of Attorney for Healthcare, remember the importance of a regular Power of Attorney. This simple document not only smooths the way of anyone trying to conduct business for you when you are flat on your back in the hospital, it can be of great help should you find yourself quite healthy, but stranded in a foreign country and needing a trusted person back home to tend to important matters for you. See a sample of this document on p. 114.

A health care proxy law allows you to appoint someone you trust—for example, a family member or close friend—to decide about treatment if you lose the ability to decide for yourself. You can do this by using a Health Care Proxy form like the one on p. 115, to appoint your "health care agent."

This law gives you the power to make sure that health care professionals follow your wishes. Your agent can also decide how your wishes apply as your medical condition changes. Hospitals, doctors, and other health care providers must follow your agent's decisions as if they were your own. You can give the person you choose as little or as much authority as you wish. You can allow that person to decide about all issues regarding health care or only specific treatments. Whatever instructions you give, that person must do as you say. Check with your state laws on health care proxy rules and regulations.

These important documents are relatively quick and easy to create. The difficult part is getting you started on the process. Like every other aspect of our deaths, the paperwork is easy to put off; however, it is a great bonus to have behind us. Think of all the problems and hassles you are sparing your loved ones by attending to as many things in advance as possible.

Remember to keep all originals and extra copies of legal documents in a safe place and filed appropriately. Having all files organized before a death occurs will make it easier on the survivor.

Everyone should apply for a major charge card in their name only in order to establish credit for them as an individual. This will come in handy in the event you need to make a large purchase.

As another piece of financial advice, make sure you have money in a separate account, in your name only, to live on in case of an unexpected death. I had a small account set aside for my daughter that got us by in the beginning. Everything was listed in both our names and, when Leo died, all accounts became "frozen." It takes awhile for them to "thaw out" so, if possible, have some extra money set aside.

When a death occurs, family members may question their loved ones' cause of death. As a method of conclusively establishing the cause of death, an autopsy may be performed to confirm diagnosis. An autopsy is a medical examination of a body after death to determine the cause of death or to investigate the extent and nature of changes caused by disease. Autopsies involve detailed examination of both the exterior and interior of the body. Once the abdominal cavity is exposed, organs are removed for examination of their internal structure, and small samples may be taken for later analysis. After the autopsy is completed, organs not needed for further study are replaced in the body cavity and all incisions are closed.

An autopsy may be performed for legal or official reasons or as part of a hospital's teaching or research program. Sometimes, the deceased's family will request an autopsy to determine whether genetic or infectious conditions led to death or to help resolve questions about possible malpractice. As in Leo's death, an autopsy was performed to see what caused his aneurysm. The report indicated that a blood vessel had weakened and finally erupted. Except when required by law, an autopsy can be performed only after the next of kin's consent is obtained or when the deceased has donated his or her body for autopsy under the provisions of the Uniform Anatomical Gift Act. You will find an "Authority for Autopsy" form on p. 116.

Another issue to consider is that of organ and tissue donation. The miracle of organ and tissue transplantation saves or greatly improves the lives of thousands of men, women, and children. Transplantation is one of the most remarkable success stories in the history of medicine. It is often the only hope for thousands of people suffering from organ failure or in desperate need of corneas, skin, bone, or other tissue. Improved surgical techniques and new anti-rejection drugs now permit successful transplantation of organs and tissues, such as heart, lung, kidney, liver, pancreas, cornea, bone, skin, and other soft tissues. More than 50,000 Americans await life-saving organs while hundreds of thousands more could benefit from tissue transplants. Tragically, the need for donated organs and tissues is greater than the supply. Thousands of people die needlessly each year due to lack of donors. According to the Coalition on Donation, every three hours someone in this country dies because of the shortage of donor organs and every eighteen minutes another person's name is added to the list of thousands who await lifesaving organ transplants. Thousands more await life-enhancing tissue transplants.

You can save lives by deciding to be an organ and tissue donor. Sharing your decision to be an organ and tissue donor with your family is as important as making the decision itself. On p. 117, you will find a sample donor card as well as organ and transplant programs to contact for further questions.

Perhaps the most important step in planning for your own death is adjusting to the concept that we will no longer have control. Many of us are motivated to take care of things that relate to our deaths because we are controllers in life and feel driven to exercise any control possible during and after our deaths. Those of us who are compulsive controllers in life have an additional learning assignment as we plan our deaths. Death is about surrendering control. Remember, the world will continue to turn even without our guidance and control.

That Men Should Fear

Cowards die many times before their death;
The valiant never taste of death but once.
Of all the wonders that I yet have heard
It seems to me most strange that men should fear;
Seeing that death, a necessary end,
will come when it will come.
— William Shakespeare (from *Julius Ceasar*)

THE LIVING WILL

Death is as much a reality as birth, growth, maturity, and old age. It is the one certainty of life. If the time comes when I, _____, can no longer take part in decisions for my own future, let this statement stand as an expression of my wishes, while I am still of sound mind. If the situation should arise in which there is no reasonable expectation of my recovery from physical or mental disability, I request that I be allowed to die and not be kept alive by artificial means or heroic measures. I do, however, ask that medication be mercifully administered to me to alleviate suffering even though this may shorten my remaining life. This statement is made after careful consideration and is in accordance with my strong convictions and beliefs. I want the wishes and directions here expressed carried out to the extent permitted by law. Insofar as they are not legally enforceable, I hope that those to whom this Will is addressed will regard them as morally bound by these provisions.

Signed _____
Date _____
Witness _____
Witness _____

Copies of this request have been given to _____

_____

_____

_____

Concern for Dying, New York, NY

POWER OF ATTORNEY

State of _____

County of _____

WITNESSETH, that I, the undersigned, being of sound and disposing mind and memory, and as my own free wish and deed, have made, constituted and appointed, and by these presents do hereby make, constitute and appoint _____ to be my true and lawful attorney, to represent me in all matters, giving and granting unto my said attorney, full power and authority to do and perform every act and deed whatsoever requisite and necessary to be done in and about my properties and affairs, as fully and to all intents and purposes as I might or could do if physically able and present, with full power of substitution and revocation, and also for me and in my name, as my act and deed, to sign, seal, execute and deliver all legal documents and instruments in writing and to sign my name for me to all my checks, receipts and all other legal or necessary acknowledgments and papers of whatever kind and nature, hereby ratifying and confirming all that my said attorney, _____, shall lawfully do or cause to be done by virtue hereof.

IN WITNESS WHEREOF, I have hereunto set my hand this _____ day of _____, 20____.

_____

ATTEST:

_____

_____

Before me this day personally appeared _____, who signed the above instrument and acknowledged that she/he did so for the purposes therein expressed.

Witness my hand and official seal this _____ day of _____, 20____.

_____
Notary Public
My commission expires:

HEALTH CARE PROXY

1. I, _____
hereby appoint (name, address and telephone number)

_____
_____

As my health care agent to make any and all health care decisions for me, except to the extent that I state otherwise. This proxy will take effect when and if I become unable to make my own health care decisions.

2. Optional instructions: I direct my proxy to make health care decisions in accord with my wishes and limitations as stated below, or as he or she otherwise knows. (Attach additional pages if necessary.)

_____
_____

(Unless your agent knows your wishes about artificial nutrition and hydration [feeding tubes], your agent will not be allowed to make decisions about artificial nutrition and hydration.)

3. Names of substitute or fill-in-proxy if the person I appoint above is unable, unwilling or unavailable to act as my health care agent (name, address and telephone number).

_____
_____

4. Unless I revoke it, this proxy will remain in effect indefinitely, or until the date or conditions stated below. This proxy will expire

_____.

5. Signature _____
   Address _____
   _____
   Date _____

Statement by Witnesses (must be at least 18 years of age)

I declare that the person who signed this document is personally known to me and appears to be of sound mind and acting of his or her own free will. He or she signed this document in my presence.

Witness _____

Witness _____

AUTHORITY FOR AUTOPSY

_____ Date _____ Hour _____.M.

Hospital_____

The undersigned hereby authorize the above named hospital to permit its Pathologist, and/or such doctors and assistants as he may desire, to perform an autopsy and complete post-mortem examination upon the body of _____,
deceased, including the taking of tissues for special study and microscopic examination, for the purpose of determining the exact cause of death.

Witnesses: Signed _____

_____   Relationship _____

_____   Signed _____

                                  Relationship _____

ORGAN & TISSUE DONATION

This is a legal document under the Uniform Anatomical Gift Act or similar laws, signed by the donor and the following two witnesses in the presence of each other.

_____
Donor's signature

_____   _____
Donor's date of birth   City & State

_____   _____
Witness   Witness

_____   _____
Next of kin   Telephone

This is to inform you that I have pledged the Gift of Life. At my death, please honor my wishes by telling my doctors and nurses that I have talked with you about organ and tissue donation. In the hope that I may help others after my death, I pledge this gift for transplanation, medical study or education.

I give: _____ Any needed organs/tissues
        _____ Only the following organs/tissues

_____

_____
Specify the organ(s)/tissue(s)

_____

_____
Limitations or special wishes if any

_____
Donor's signature

To Remember Me

Give my sight to the man who has never seen a sunrise, a baby's face or love in the eyes of a woman.

Give my heart to a person whose own heart has caused nothing but endless days of pain.

Give my blood to the teen-ager who was pulled from the wreckage of his car, so that he might live to see his grandchildren play.

Give my kidneys to one who depends on a machine to exist from week to week.

Take my bones, every muscle, every fiber and nerve in my body and find a way to make a crippled child walk.

If you must bury something, let it be my faults, my weaknesses and all prejudice against my fellow man.

Give my sins to the devil.

Give my soul to God.

If, by chance, you wish to remember me, do it with a kind deed or word to someone who needs you.

If you do all I have asked I will live forever.

— Author Unknown

LEGAL GUIDELINES AFTER A DEATH OCCURS

The following information contains specific facts to help one make the best decisions at the time of loss and to understand later reactions.

Collect all necessary papers in order to file for various benefits and to finalize the estate. You will need copies of the death certificate to give to agencies you contact. Some offices will accept a photocopy but you may need certified copies which you can purchase for a few dollars. These are available through your funeral director or the county health department. You will need the Social Security number of the deceased, the spouse, and the children. In addition, you will need copies of all insurance policies, a certificate of honorable discharge (if the deceased was a veteran), a marriage certificate, birth certificates of dependent children, your Will, and a complete list of all property, including stocks, bonds, savings accounts, personal property and real estate.

Check to see if the deceased has any of the following types of insurance policies:

- life insurance
- accident insurance
- automobile insurance
- mortgage or loan insurance
- credit card insurance
- insurance provided by the employer of the deceased

If the deceased paid into Social Security for at least forty quarters, he or she is considered to be covered. Check with your local Social Security office to determine if the deceased is eligible. There are two types of benefits—a death benefit of $255.00 toward burial expenses and survivors' benefits for a spouse or children.

Check with the local Veterans Administration office to determine if you or any dependent children are eligible for benefits. Veterans are also eligible for some funeral arrangements regarding plots and grave markers (and possible eligibility for a military funeral).

The deceased may be eligible for employee benefits if employed at the time of death. This may include a final paycheck for vacation or sick leave. If the death was work-related, there may even be workman's compensation benefits. Also, check about union membership or retirement pensions.

Hopefully, the deceased has a valid Will. Probate is the legal process of distributing the estate of the deceased to the rightful heirs. This consists of the following steps:

- appointment of an individual by the court to act as a personal representative or "executor" of the estate. This person is often named in the Will. If there is no Will, the court will appoint a personal representative, usually the spouse or a relative.
- Proving that the Will, if it exists, is valid.
- Informing interested parties, especially heirs and beneficiaries, that the Will is being probated.
- Disposing of the estate by the executor in accordance with the Will or the laws of the state.

If you do not know already, find out if the deceased had a safety deposit box. If the box was rented only in the name of the deceased, it will require a court order to open the box. Only the Will or any other materials pertaining to the death can be removed until the Will has been probated.

The federal and state income taxes are due for the year following the death of the deceased. The spouse may file jointly for this year. If children are involved, the spouse may file jointly for two additional years. Contact your local IRS office for the booklet "Information for Survivors, Executors and Administrators."

You may need to revise documents after a death by changing title on property or transferring ownership. These may include:

- insurance policies
- will
- bank accounts
- stocks and bonds
- credit cards
- mortgage or other loans
- title to house
- title to car

Let me suggest that you do not immediately make permanent significant financial decisions about moving, selling your home, or changing jobs. I almost sold my home and moved out of state. I now realize I made the right choice by staying put. This time is needed to consider your situation before making decisions responsibly. You may later regret rushing into a decision.

It might be wise at this time to have an advisor for your financial and legal problems. Don't think you can do it all yourself. Few people can truly function at their best for a minimum of six months. It is closer to two years before one functions at his normal level of performance.

Contact a professional if you need services—particularly a lawyer, financial advisor, or a mental health counselor. There are many programs developed to provide assistance and support to the newly widowed.

Be sure to advise your family of your decisions and the arrangements you have made. Knowing everything is taken care of will give both you and your family peace of mind.

FACING DEATH

Death is a subject that is usually avoided, ignored, and denied by our society, yet death and dying are an integral part of human existence. Death is inevitable for all of us, and should not be ignored until loved ones or friends die. It is very important that we understand the subject of death and try to grasp its meaning in order to lead healthier and happier lives. The purpose of this section is to help the reader accept the inevitability of death and become aware that death is a natural ending to life, rather than something to fear or deny. If one learns more about death, one will become more aware of the value of life and live it to the fullest.

> So death, the most terrifying of ills, is nothing to us, since so long as we exist. It does not then concern either the living or the dead, since for the former it is not and the latter are no more.
> — Epicurus

The formation of attitudes begins very early and goes on throughout one's life. We can change our attitudes at any period through formal education, through changes in our behavior, and if the desire is strong enough, through sheer effort of will. Not many of us do this—we go along believing what we learned years ago—never questioning. Unless we examine, question, and change our attitudes about death, we cannot become fully developed persons. We cannot achieve identity or selfhood. In the absence of death education, we still managed to learn about it and usually at a very early age. The concern here, however, is the misinformation, the unhealthy attitudes, and the false facts—not to mention the fears that people accumulate between childhood and adulthood. Our nation is committed to good education—universally available—but not good death education. Why?

We've always had poor death education as known to us in the many nursery rhymes we learned as children, such as in "Old Mother Hubbard's" second verse:

> She went to the baker's
> To buy him some bread.
> And when she came back
> The poor dog was dead.

or what about poor Cock Robin?

> "Who killed Cock Robin?"
> "I," said the sparrow,
> "With my bow and arrow.
> "I killed Cock Robin."

Children learn about death in fairy tales such as Humpty Dumpty and Sleeping Beauty, through television, and even in a child's prayer such as, "If I should die before I wake, I pray the Lord my soul to take." They learn about death when a pet dies. The child finds dead bugs and dead birds. We teach him what we learned: fears, anxieties, doubts, denials, and repressions.

Most of us actually enjoy life and we are hesitant to even consider leaving it. We have our fears, but the sad thing is that most of our fears about death and dying are unnecessary and can easily be resolved.

Let us try to conquer these fears through mature consideration. First, we have certain superstitions about death and we are often frightened by the idea of haunted houses and spirits of the dead. But how many of us have actually confronted a ghost or goblin?

Second, we fear our own death because we know that it may grab us when we least expect it to—with unfinished business to take care of. It is extremely difficult for most of us to carry on our daily activities with the constant fear that tomorrow may never come. We really need to accept the fact that we can never accomplish everything ourselves because death will eventually overtake us and someone else will have to complete our unfinished tasks. If we can only understand this then death cannot take us by surprise.

When we think of dying we often visualize a painful death and we fear that we will die alone. Do we really need these fears? Many of us fear death because we want to live forever. Yet we have always known that without death, life becomes unbearable. What would it be like to live in a world where death did not occur? Eventually we would suffocate from being overcrowded!

What could death education contribute to the art of living? I personally believe that death education can alleviate the fears associated with death so we can live fuller lives. The subject of death is negative in our eyes because we perceive it as an end instead of a beginning. But actually death is an extension of the life process: Birth – – – Life – – – Death.

Normally, we don't like to face the issue of death, but death can be welcome in the event of a terminal illness where there has been much pain and suffering. It is often considered a curse when the victim is young. In this case, we fight against it and deny it, which results in anger, shock, and disbelief.

But, what really causes our fear of death? The fear of not knowing what happens seems to be the most popular response. Some fear losing control or becoming a burden to their loved ones while others fear being judged in this life or in the hereafter.

It is not death that is the source of all our evils, and of a mean and cowardly spirit, but rather the fear of death.
— Epictetus (Greek philosopher)

Today scientists actually study death—a science called thanatology—to better understand what death is. These scientists report that we need to be aware of what happens when the body dies. A number of things occur: muscles change and become stiff—the stage of rigor mortis, which lasts about thirty-six hours. The skin becomes cold due to lack of circulation. Then decomposition of the body results because tissues die. Different things take place at various stages of death. Clinical death usually occurs first—when the heart and lungs cease to function. This causes brain cells to die if the person is not revived. Sometimes clinical death can be reversed through cardiopulmonary resuscitation, electric stimuli, and heart massage. Recovery can occur although brain damage may result. Without oxygen from the blood, brain cells begin to die in approximately four minutes. The doctors use an electroencephalogram (EEG) to test for brain waves. Brain death is a medical diagnosis made by the doctor which includes the following criteria:

- total lack of movement or breathing
- total unawareness and unresponsiveness to stimuli
- total absence of reflexes

Before declaring that brain death has occurred, two possible causes must be ruled out: hypothermia and drug overdose, because these conditions can be treated with a chance of complete recovery.

Biological death (also known as cellular death) is the next stage in the dying process. After brain death occurs, eventually all organs cease to function. This process is irreversible. The brain is dead, but some organs, as in the case of Leo, remain alive for short periods until all the oxygen is depleted. The tissues and organs then begin to die. One's hair and fingernails may continue to grow for approximately twenty-four hours.

Legal death is pronounced by a doctor when there is total unresponsiveness by means of several examinations.

Psychological death should be recognized as a stage of the dying process. This stage involves unresponsiveness to one's environment as in a coma.

Theological death refers to when the soul leaves the physical body as some religions believe; however, this stage technically cannot be measured.

What happens after death? Is it all over? Is that all there is? How we feel about life after death is determined by our personal and religious beliefs. Most religions believe in some kind of afterlife. For example, Christianity, Islam, Judaism, and Hinduism all stress the immortality of one's spirit, while believing that the flesh is mortal. The Hindus also believe the spirit inhabits new life and is reincarnated. Christian and Islamic beliefs are centered around the resurrection of bodies and souls. A belief in immortality, whatever one's religion, could reduce the fear of death.

Philosophers and theologians the worlds over have expressed their views about the existence of a soul. The soul is described as a spiritual part of a person, as opposed to a physical part which continues to live after the body dies.

The heaven/hell concept of life after death is a widespread belief with heaven depicted as a blissful or good place and hell as a bad place—associated with fire and suffering. Many Christians generally believe that heaven is where believers share in eternal life with God and hell is where sinners go—a destiny for the damned.

In the last few years, studies have been conducted of people who have been pronounced clinically dead but were revived and then related their "dying experience." Some experiences of those near death include: feelings of being outside their body, bright lights, going through tunnels and gates, and seeing persons who died earlier. According to Dr. Raymond Moody, the author of *Life After Life*, many individuals found it difficult to describe their experiences in conventional terms but most were considered pleasant.

> Death is psychologically as important as birth. Shrinking away from it is something unhealthy and abnormal which robs the second half of life of its purpose.
>
> — Carl Jung (Psychologist)

In summary, there is no need to be afraid of death for it is the denial of death that is somewhat responsible for people living empty, meaningless lives. Take this time to think about your own death. How much time and energy have you put into examining your inner self—your beliefs, feelings, hopes, and fears about the end of your time on earth. If there are things you need to do to make your life more personally meaningful before you die, do them now. Don't wait until you get the first notice, for you may not have the energy to do them then. We are painfully aware that someday we will die. Each day we live brings us closer to the reality of it. Throughout our life, people die among us, and deep in our unconscious is the knowledge that it will also happen to us. We should not fear this—to be fearful of life is like a "living death." If you live your life fully, you need not fear the end. By dying we promote the life of others to be born to live their days in this world as we have—to give a part of them to be remembered by.

I hope this overview will encourage my readers to engage in important self-examination regarding their personal views about death.

> Let us deprive death of its strangeness, let us frequent it, let us get used to it; let us have nothing more often in mind than death. We do not know where death awaits us; so let us wait for it everywhere. To practice death is to practice freedom. A person who has learned how to die has unlearned how to be a slave.
> — Montaigne, French philosopher (1533-1592)

> Lord, make me a channel of thy peace—
> That where there is hatred, I may bring love—
> That where there is wrong, I may bring the
>   spirit of forgiveness—
> That where there is discord, I may bring
>   harmony—
> That where there is error, I may bring truth—
> That where there is despair, I may bring hope—
> That where there are shadows, I may bring light—
> That where there is sadness, I may bring joy.
> Lord, grant that I may seek
> Rather to comfort than be comforted—
> To understand, than to be understood—
> To love, than to be loved.
> For it is by self-forgetting that one finds.
> It is by forgiving that one is forgiven.
> It is by dying that one awakens to eternal life.
>   St. Francis

Togetherness

Death is nothing at all. I have only slipped away into the next room.

Whatever we were to each, that we are still. Call me by my old familiar name, speak to me in the easy way which you always used.

Laugh as we always laughed at the little jokes we enjoyed together. Play, smile, think of me—pray for me.

Let my name be the household word that it always was. Let it be spoken without effort.

Life means all that it ever meant. It is the same as it ever was. There is absolutely unbroken continuity.

Why should I be out of your mind because I am out of your sight?

I am waiting for you, for an interval somewhere very near—just around the corner.

All is well. Nothing is lost.

One brief moment and all will be as it was before—only better, infinitely happier and forever—we will all, one day, be one together with Christ.

—Author Unknown

There Is No Death

I am standing upon the seashore.
A ship at my side, spreads her white sails to the morning breeze,
and starts for the blue ocean.
She is an object of beauty and strength,
and I stand and watch her,
until at length,
she hangs like a speck of white cloud,
just where the sea and the sky come to mingle with each other.
Then someone at my side says,
"There! She's gone!"
Gone from my sight, that's all.
She is just as large in mast and hull and spar as she was when she left my side,
and she is just as able to bear her load of living weight to her destined port.

Her diminished size is in me,
not in her.
And just at the moment when someone at my side says,
"There! She's gone!
There are other eyes watching her coming,
and other voices ready to take up the glad shout.
"There she comes!" And that is dying.

—Author Unknown

The Elephant in the Room

There's an elephant in the room.
It is large and squatting, so it is hard to get around it.
Yet we squeeze by with "How are you?" And "I'm fine . . ."
And a thousand other forms of trivial chatter.
We talk about the weather.
We talk about work.
We talk about everything else—except the elephant in the room.
We all know it is there.
We are thinking about the elephant as we talk.
It is constantly on our minds,
For you see, it is a very big elephant.
But we do not talk about the elephant in the room.
Oh, please, say her name.
Oh, please, say "Barbara" again.
Oh, please, let's talk about the elephant in the room.
For if we talk about her death,
Perhaps we can talk about her life.
Can I say "Barbara" and not have you look away?
For if I cannot, you are leaving me
Alone . . . In a room . . .
With an elephant.

— Author Unknown

My first experience with the death of a human (as opposed to an animal) was actually an interesting one. I don't know that my mother realized at the time what an awesome job she was doing at providing me with a wonderful foundation for grief and loss to carry with me in the back of my mind through the inevitable losses that accompany us though life. I was about seven years old. My mother is French and we would travel to France almost every year to visit relatives. On this particular occasion we visited one of mothers' great aunts who I had never before met. She was from my perspective and understanding not feeling well. When we arrived at her apartment, she was in bed, but able to talk and interact with us. She spoke no English . . . only French and Polish. Well, as all good little girls who are raised by European parents can do, I could sing various songs in Polish and French. Of course, my mother made me "perform" some of these for this ill relative. I sang about three songs and with each song this aunt just smiled and laughed and clapped her hands. She couldn't believe that a little American girl could sing such songs so beautifully in Polish and French. We stayed for a little while and then went back to our hotel.

The next day we received a call from the aunt's son. He told my mother that this aunt had died in the night. My mother told me this and said that we were going to go there to see her. See her, I asked? Yes, see her. My mother explained to me that in Europe they keep the body in the bed at home after the person dies. So we went to her house. There she was . . . lying in bed looking as if she were taking a snooze. We walked into the room . . . me, close by my mother's side. I looked at this woman in the bed and she looked very yellow. My mother explained to me that this is what happens when a person dies and the blood is no longer flowing through their body. She also explained that the reason people don't look like that in America when they die and we see them in a coffin in the funeral home is because there are people whose job it is to put makeup on them and bring color to their face so they look the way we remember them when they were alive. My mother also explained that there is ice packed around the body to preserve it for a couple of days while friends and family come to visit. She told me that I could touch this aunt (which I chose not to). My mother touched her and told me that she felt cold and that there was nothing to be afraid of . . . that this was a natural thing and that the aunt had been very sick and we were lucky to have gotten to see her before she died. Around this time the aunt's son came in the room and told my mom that I had made his mother's last moments happy and full of laughter by singing my songs to her.

This experience has stayed with me my whole life and has been a ray of light in so many ways. My mother showed me that death is a natural part of life. I also learned at an early age that literally someone can be here today and gone tomorrow. My mother also taught me with this experience that the body is simply a housing or a "suit" that we wear for our soul . . . and that the body dies but the soul or spirit or life force goes on . . . in memories. My mother had no idea, according to her, that she was giving me such an incredible gift. Her reaction and response to this death experience with me on this trip to Europe was simply natural. I still thank her from time to time for this gift and remind her how remarkable she was and still is.

— Lisa Kiebzak

EXPLAINING DEATH TO A CHILD

Childhood is a very special time of life—but during this time children as well as adults will eventually have some kind of confrontation with death. It is at this time that children need to be supported and encouraged by those they interact with on a daily basis.

Our responses to death experiences as an adult are based on the losses that we experienced as a child and those we were influenced by during this vulnerable period of our life. These early experiences of childhood play a large part in deciding how a child perceives herself and the world around them.

Today, fewer people die at an early age so the child has little or no experience with the death of relatives because they grow old or become ill and are placed in a nursing home or hospital. It is up to the child's parents or guardian to provide an opportunity for them to effectively cope with death. The purpose of this chapter in my book is to teach one how to explain death to a child and to help that child cope with grief, personal loss, and emotional stress following the death of a loved one. Whether the death is sudden or anticipated, violent or peaceful, untimely or at the end of a long period of suffering, externally caused or self-inflicted, the results can be quite devastating in the mind of a child.

When someone important to a child dies, there is no easy way to explain what has happened. Words like, "gone," "in Heaven," "with God," don't always explain the absence of someone's presence—especially to a child. Children understand life in different ways at different ages. The breakdown of the age groups are two- to five-year-olds (preschool), ages nine to twelve, and teenagers. Their ages, level of maturity, relationship to the deceased and, in some cases, personality, will depend on what and how much you tell the child.

Normally, a preschool child has some understanding of "here" and "not here." For instance, peek-a-boo is a popular game because out-of-sight-but-not-out-of-mind is developing at this age. Nonliving things are usually in the back of their mind; whereas, living things are much more important to them. A preschool child does not understand death or the permanence of it. It is just not real to them. Something can live and then die to a child of this age or vice versa. For example, cartoon characters can get smashed totally flat and get up again as if nothing ever happened to them. Children tend to deny death as a final process at this age. They don't know what "being dead" really means. To a young child death is a temporary state.

A good place to begin explaining death is with samples of nature. Explain how flowers, leaves, and bugs are first born, how they grow and, finally, how they die. Preschoolers are aware of this life cycle. They are not threatening to their everyday life and can be used to explain the terms "living" and "dead." A good source for this is *The Fall of Freddie the Leaf*, by Leo Buscaglia (1982). It tells the story of how Freddie the leaf experiences the changing seasons along with his companion leaves. He learns about the delicate balance between life and death. Some children at this age may have experienced the death of a pet so this event could be used to explain the death of a relative or friend. One might say "Grandma's body stopped working" and then go on to explain that she was very sick or, in most cases, very old. One should never tell a child that the deceased is "just sleeping" because the child may be afraid to go to sleep at night. By not telling the child the truth is denying the reality of the death and this can cause much confusion for the child later on. Most importantly, never tell your child something they will have to unlearn at a later time. They may lose trust and respect in you.

Between the ages of five and nine the child has heard of death but may be confused with the terminology associated with it. A child of this age may understand what death is but they may think it's reversible as in the case of many cartoons. Death is often personified—as someone who comes and takes you away. Children, at this age, know death exists but attempt to keep it at a distance. The main concern of most parents of a child this age is whether or not to include the child in the funeral services. Adults should keep in mind that the goal is to understand the child's feelings and to help. One must remember not to judge the child. Each child is a unique person and deserves respect. According to Wolfelt (1983) "the development of a nonjudgmental attitude toward children when they experience a death in their lives, also involves recognizing that at times they will ask questions that may be shocking or seem irrelevant to adults. The ability of the adult to respond to questions without demonstrating shock or embarrassment aids the child in experiencing a sense of empathy and respect" p. 14. Associated with this nonjudgmental attitude is accepting the child's ability to participate in the events following the death—attending the wake, viewing the body, going to the funeral, and visiting the grave. Remembering that each child is unique, these choices will vary according to the age and/or maturity of the child. A child needs to express grief and to know that their reactions are acceptable. Children of this age may think death is contagious and will avoid other children whose parents have died. This child may suffer severe loneliness if constant reassurance from family members is not given. These children need details—biological causes for the death, information about the funeral, and explanations about what will follow the funeral. They need clear answers to their questions and how to answer those questions that other people may ask.

When a child is between nine and twelve years of age he or she knows that you live and then you die. They know that death is final but they may still be somewhat confused. This age group may feel responsible for what happens to them or around them. The child may feel he caused the death—there is usually a great deal of guilt associated with death. The parent must talk to the child and help him or her understand how the person died and assure the child that they are not responsible in any way for the person's death. At this age the child may think of the death as a punishment for bad behavior of the deceased. The parent must explain what happened physically because if reasons are left unexplained the child may think the deceased caused his own death by doing something wrong or that they themselves are responsible for the death by not taking action to prevent it. Parents are encouraged to tell the truth at all times. Even if all the details are unknown, answer the questions in the best way you can—admit when you don't know the answers. Let the child know that death is difficult for anyone to talk about and very hard to understand. Assure the child that you will do your best to help them understand what has happened. By being available to the child you can help him work through his or her grief.

As for teenagers, this is also a time of emotional conflict so it is extremely important that this group be assured of their own self-worth. They see death as inevitable for all of us. They know death is final and irreversible. It is the cessation of all biological functioning. For the teen, guilt and anger are common feelings following the death of a close one. Teenagers view death as the end of one's relationship with the world that they have known and the rebirth into a world of eternal life, love, hope, and faith in God. A teenager and an adult experience the same process of grieving. They both need time to adjust and, if the period of grieving lasts too long, professional help may be necessary. Symptoms might include delinquency, not willing to remain in school, tardiness, learning difficulties, withdrawal, excessive anger, unfriendliness, not communicating, suspicion, or even sexual perversion. Elisabeth Kübler-Ross (1983) stresses how important it is not to shelter our children from death and dying. Our intent is to protect them from harm but, in actuality, we are depriving them of a very improtant part of life. By keeping children separated from those who are dying or who have died, we instill unnecessary fear in them.

Death is difficult to understand for any child but, as parents, it is our responsibility to discuss the subject of death with our children. Forcing a child to deal with death your way or exposing him or her to death when they are not ready can greatly harm them at a later time in life. Those who learn to know death, rather than fear it, become teachers about life.

Leaves of Grass—"Great Are the Myths"

Great is life . . . and the real and mystical . . .
Great is death . . . Surely as life holds all parts
    together, death holds all parts together;
Sure as the stars return again after they merge
    in the light, death is as great as life.

                              — Walt Whitman (poet)

While I thought I was learning how to live, I have been learning
how to die.

                              — Leonardo da Vinci

HOW TO HELP YOUR CHILD REDUCE
STRESS WHILE GRIEVING

1. Let your child know that all family relationships have not changed but have simply altered.
2. Seek opportunities for the love of your child to be shared by other family members.
3. Express your love to your child as often as possible.
4. Spend quality time with your child—one-on-one experience.
5. Avoid changing familiar surroundings and friends. Let your child stay in the same school for the remainder of the school year if at all possible.
6. Try to follow the familiar routine of daily life by avoiding changes that may affect your child.
7. Accept your child's way of grieving if it appears different from your own.
8. Give your child time to grieve, for often there is a delayed reaction to grief in children.
9. Encourage your child to express feelings of sadness and anger. Respond to their fear with reassurance and comfort them.
10. Let your child know that she was not the cause of her other parent's death.
11. Talk about the absent parent to your child. Keep the memories alive.
12. Avoid delegating additional responsibilities to your child.
13. Listen to your child when she talks to you. Maintain eye contact as well.
14. Hug your child often.
15. Read to the child whenever possible—relaxing together is important.

16. Do not take your anger and frustration out on your child.
17. Look for any unusual behavioral change in your child and inform your pediatrician.
18. Continue to celebrate as a family on holidays.
19. Look to the future with a positive attitude so that your child will follow your example of coping with courage and confidence.
20. Be honest with your child about how the death occurred. Do not use phrases such as "They are just sleeping," or "passed on," as this may cause confusion. Use the words "died" and "dead."
21. Read books on children's grief and the adult mourning process to help you understand the grief process in the mind of a child.
22. Allow your child to go to the cemetery if they wish.
23. Give your child the choice of attending the Wake and funeral procession. It is important to encourage them to go and be a part of the ceremony, do not force them!
24. Openly grieve in front of the child. Cry! And give the child permission to cry!
25. Love your child unconditionally.

Do you know the sensation of being a child and being alone? Children can adapt wonderfully to specific fears, like a pain, a sickness, or a death. It is the unknown which is truly terrifying for them. They have no fund of knowledge in how the world operates, and so they feel completely vulnerable (Katzenbach, 1986, p. 322).

IMPORTANT POINTS TO REMEMBER

Some people grow stronger from their experiences of grief. These people emerge from their losses with new strength, abilities, and inner beauty. Good grief requires time, patience, suffering, self-trust, courage, and hope. It doesn't happen all at once and it certainly isn't easy. But when it happens, it is truly wonderful.

Survivors of grief have reported several ways that have helped them transform painful losses into personal growth. I now share them with you.

1. Express your feelings in helpful, non-hurtful ways—through music, poetry, drawing, screaming, nature walks, journal writing, punching pillows, and talking to others.
2. Realize no two people travel the same road to grief. You are a unique individual and so is your experience with grief.

3. Just as your experience with death is different from others, so is your period of mourning. Everyone reacts differently to death.
4. Be aware that you will experience mood swings and periods of depression. These emotions will pass in time.
5. Preserve the memories of your loved one. A person may die, but the memories of that relationship will live forever.
6. Remember you are still the same person you were before and just as important even though your loved one is no longer with you.
7. Be patient.
8. Allow yourself to suffer.
9. Feel your feelings.
10. Let your friends and relatives know how you want to be treated—especially if you need to be alone.
11. Share your feelings with a close friend.
12. Get out and do things. Don't let sadness overcome you. Involve yourself. If at first you don't succeed, try, try again.
13. Let nature take its course.
14. Never compare your healing progress to someone else. Remember you and your experiences are unique.
15. Deal with unfinished business.
16. Seek and offer forgiveness.
17. Consult your friends if you need a helping hand. They are there to guide you and keep you strong.
18. Hug someone every day. The more hugs the better!
19. Keep yourself busy—especially on those special days, such as birthdays, anniversaries, and holidays. Have loved ones around you as much as possible. But remember not to overwork yourself.
20. Help others, for it will give meaning to your own life.
21. Be aware that there will always be a void that only time will heal.
22. Know that your present suffering promotes growth.
23. Do not make any major decisions during the first year unless absolutely necessary.
24. Refrain from using alcohol or drugs to numb your pain.
25. If you feel you need outside assistance, support groups can be helpful in restoring your self-confidence. Learning from others with similar experiences can help relieve the pain.
26. If you feel you need one-on-one counseling instead, contact a professional or visit your clergyman.

27. An education on grief will not "make things better." You have to live through every moment before you heal. It does get better.
28. Repeat positive affirmations to yourself each day such as, "I know things will get better" or "I will survive."
29. Be aware that your status as a "single person" may be perceived as a threat to another's marriage.
30. Do not let your children (or anyone else!) control your life. When you are ready to date, it should be your decision. We all need adult companionship.
31. Understand that you are likely to face other losses while working through your grief work—hopefully, not as traumatic.
32. Be aware of your own progress in grieving the death of your loved one. Identify tools for coping which may help you in the future.
33. Listen to your inner feelings by trusting your own insights. Ignore advice from others if you do not agree with them. Do what *you* feel is right. If you must take advice, let it be from those who are trained to give it.
34. Look for the humor in things—even though it hurts.
35. Take care of yourself.
36. Say your "goodbyes" without burning bridges behind you.
37. Have quiet times for remembering your loved one.

When someone you love has died, you tend to recall best those few moments and incidents that helped to clarify your sense, not of the person who has died, but of your own self. And if you loved the person a great deal . . . your sense of who you are will have been clarified many times, and so you will have many such moments to remember

— Banks, 1991, p. 43

Her Journey's Just Begun

Don't think of her as gone away—
her journey's just begun,
Life holds so many facets—this earth is only one.
Just think of her as resting
from the sorrows and the tears
in a place of warmth and comfort

where there are no days and years.
Think how she must be wishing
that we could know today
how nothing but our sadness
can really pass away.
And think of her as living
in the hearts of those she touched . . .
for nothing loved is ever lost—
and she was loved so much.

—Author Unknown

EPILOGUE

Although the journey I traveled through grief was a road full of bumps and pitfalls, I did recover, and that is what matters most of all. I know it makes no difference whether you die at a young age or old age. What is important is how you lived the years you had. Leo's death promoted my growth—to do things I never dreamed of doing. I realize now those pitfalls were just setbacks in my life as a way of testing my endurance. I learned some very important things through my grief work. Death is no longer a taboo subject with me.

Through this experience I have learned that, should I ever find myself in this situation again, I will survive. The pain and suffering from the loss will be there but I will know what to expect. I have learned more about myself—how I handle tragedy, how I find strength, how I cope, and how intense my fears of loss are. I am stronger now and mature enough to realize that my own life is important and that I must take care of myself both physically and mentally in order to progress through grief.

I don't fear death as I once did. I have learned from those who have died before me—that there is no holding on, that we must let go. I believe that it is only our acceptance of our mortality that lets us live and appreciate the wonder of life. I know that if something does not directly affect my own life I will be able to get through it okay and I will manage the best I can. I realize now that it's not death we should fear—the fear lies in a life not lived. Once you really force yourself to understand this, the easier it will be for you to accept your own death— and the more fully you will learn to live each day here and now. It is wonderful to be alive and once you realize this you pursue your dreams and ambitions and enjoy life to the fullest. I have wept and I have mourned, but now I am alive. The time to laugh and be happy is here again.

For those of you who have not yet recovered—be patient—you will in time. You may not think so—just as I did not—but time does heal most wounds. It's just a matter of time.

> Learn from your past,
> live the here and now,
> and look forward to the future.
> — Author Unknown

We Remember Them

In the rising of the sun
  and it's going down,
    We remember them;

In the blowing of the wind
  and in the chill of winter,
    We remember them;

In the opening buds
  and in the warmth of summer,
    We remember them;

In the rustling of leaves
  and the beauty of autumn,
    We remember them;

In the beginning of the year
  and when it ends,
    We remember them;

When we are weary
  and in need of strength,
    We remember them;

When we are lost
  and sick at heart,
    We remember them;
When we have joys
  and sick at heart,
    We remember them;

When we have joys
  and yearn to share,
    We remember them;

So long as we live, they too will live,
  for they are now a part of us as
    We remember them.
                    From *Gates of Prayer*
                    Reform Judaism Prayerbook

MEANS OF SUPPORT

Support through the grieving process is crucial to recovery. The following is a list of potential resources:

Accord, Inc.
1930 Bishop Lane, #947
Louisville, KY 40218
(800) 346-3087
(literature, seminars, and workshops)

ADEC (Association for Death Education and Counseling)
638 Prospect Avenue
Hartford, CT 06015
(203) 586-7503

American Association of Retired Persons (AARP)
601 E Street, NW
Department PM
Washington, DC 20049
(provides a free pamphlet, "On Being Alone," and referrals to nationwide bereavement groups co-sponsored by AARP)

American Association of Suicidology
4201 Connecticut Avenue NW, Suite 310
Washington, DC 20008
(202) 237-2280
(an information clearinghouse that supplies literature and local referrals to survivors of suicide)

American Self-Help Clearinghouse
St. Clares-Riverside Medical Center
Denville, NJ 07834
(201) 625-7101

Animal Medical Center
New York, NY
(212) 838-8100
(pet grief)

The Beginning Experience
305 Michigan Avenue
Detroit, MI 48226
(313) 965-5110
(for bereaved spouses)

Bide-A-Wee Foundation
New York, NY
(212) 838-8100
(pet grief)

Center for Help in Time of Loss
600 Blue Hill Road
River Vale, NJ 07675
(201) 391-4473
(a nonprofit organization which holds grief recovery groups)

Center for Loss and Life Transition
3735 Broken Bow Road
Fort Collins, CO 80526
(303) 226-6050
(literature, seminars, and workshops)

Coalition on Donation
1100 Boulders Parkway, Suite 500
Richmond, VA 23255
(800) 355-SHARE
(organ donation)

Compassionate Friends
P.O. Box 1347
Oak Brook, IL 60522-3696
(312) 323-5010
(a self-help support organization for bereaved parents and siblings who have experienced the death of a child, brother, or sister — they provide brochures and referrals to support groups in one of their 650 nationwide chapters)

The Dougy Center
P.O. Box 86852
Portland, OR 97286
(503) 775-5683
(a support group for grieving children)

Grief Recovery Help Line
(800) 445-4808 — Monday through Friday — 9-5
(an educational service sponsored by the Grief Recovery Institute)

Funeral and Memorial Society of America
6900 Lost Lake Road
Egg Harbor, WI 54209
(414) 868-3136

The Hemlock Society USA
P.O. Box 101810
Denver, CO 80250-9932
(800) 247-7421 or Fax (303) 639-1224

Hospice Foundation of America
1334 G Street NW, Suite 605
Washington, DC 20005
(800) 854-3402
(offers information and a one-hour videotape entitled "Living With Grief: Personally and Professionally")

International Association for Widowed People
P.O. Box 3564
Springfield, IL 62708
(217) 787-0886
(offers programs, literature, and other resources for the widowed)

International Association of Pet cemeteries
2845 Oakcrest Place
Land O;Lakes, FL 34639
(800) 952-5541
(pet grief)

International Work Group on Death, Dying, and Bereavement
King's College
266 Epworth Avenue
London, Ontario, Canada N6A 2M3
(519) 433-3491

MADD (Mothers Against Drunk Driving)
511 East John Carpenter Freeway, Suite 700
Irving, TX 75062
(800) Get-MADD or (214) 744-6233
(support for those who have been victimized by drunken driving offenses)

National Hospice Organization
1901 North Moore Street, Suite 901
Arlington, VA 22009
(800) 658-8898
(provides brochures and referrals to local hospices, who can refer you to support services in your area)

National Organization for Victim Assistance
1757 Park Road, NW
Washington, D.C. 20010
(202) 232-6682 — 24-hour hotline or (800) TRY-NOVA
(a referral resource for local victim assistance services, and a 24-hour telephone crisis counseling service)

National SIDS Alliance
10500 Little Patuxent Parkway, #420
Columbia, MD 21044
(300) 221-SIDS (Edith McShane)
(parents of sudden infant death syndrome babies)

National Self-Help Clearinghouse
33 West 42nd Street, Room 620 N
New York, NY 10036
(212) 840-1259

National SHARE Office
Saint Joseph Health Center
Obstetrics Department
300 First Capital Drive
St. Charles, MO 63301
(314) 947-6164
(pregnancy and infant loss support)

National SHARE Office
St. Joseph Health Center
300 First Capitol Drive
Charles, MO 63301
(314) 947-6164
(support for stillborn, miscarriage, or newborn death)

National SIDS Clearinghouse
National Sudden Infant Death Syndrome Resource Center
2070 Chain Bridge Road
Vienna, VA 22182
(703) 821-8955
(a national resource for information and referrals to local organizations and support groups for those affected by sudden infant death syndrome)

New York Regional Transplant Program
475 Riverside Drive, Suite 1244
New York, NY 10115
(800) 443-8469
(organ transplant)

Parents of Murdered Children
National Headquarters
100 East Eighth Street, #B-41
Cincinnati, OH 45202
(503) 721-5683 (Nancy Ruhe-Munch)

POMC (Parents of Murdered Children)
1739 Bella Vista
Cincinnati, OH 45237
(513) 242-8025 or (513) 721-LOVE
(support for survivors of homicide)

Ray of Hope
P.O. Box 2323 (home office)
Iowa City, IA 52244
(319) 337-9890
(suicide survivors)

SHARE: Pregnancy and Infant Loss Support, Inc.
National Office
St. Joseph Health Center
300 First Capitol Drive
St. Charles, MO 63301-2893
(800) 821-6819 or (314) 947-6164
(a national mutual-help group for parents and siblings who have
experienced miscarriage, stillbirth, ectopic pregnancy, or early infant
death)

Sudden Infant Death Syndrome Alliance
1314 Bedford Avenue, Suite 210
Columbia, MD 21208
(410) 653-8226
(an alliance of organizations involved in research and services related
to sudden infant death syndrome)

Survivors of Suicide
P.O. Box 82262
Lincoln, NE 68423
(414) 442-4638
(support for survivors of suicide)

Survivors of Suicide
184 Salem Avenue (national office)
Dayton, OH 45406
(513) 223-9096

THEOS (They Help Each Other Spiritually)
717 Liberty Avenue
Pittsburgh, PA 15222
(412) 471-7779
(for young widows and widowers—has a spiritual emphasis and maintains approximately 100 chapters nationwide)

Unite, Inc.
Jeanes Hospital
7600 Central Avenue
Philadelphia, PA 19111
(support for parents grieving miscarriage, stillbirth, and infant death)

UNOS (United Network for Organ Sharing)
P.O. Box 13770
Richmond, VA 23225
(800) 243-6667

Widowed Persons Service
AARP (American Association of Retired Persons)
601 East Street, NW
Washington, DC 20049
(800) 424-3410 or (202) 434-2260
(offers programs, literature, and other resources for the widowed)

Other Sources

Crisis intervention centers
Adult activity groups
Churches
Hospitals
Community human relations services
Local newspaper
Library

Journals and Other Publications

Bereavement: A Magazine of Hope and Healing
c/o Bereavement Publishers, Inc.
8133 Telegraph Drive
Colorado Springs, CO 80920
(719) 266-0006

Death Studies
c/o Taylor and Francis
1101 Vermont Avenue NW, Suite 200
Washington, DC 20005

The Euthanasia Review
c/o Hemlock Society
P.O. Box 66218
Los Angeles, CA 90066

*The Hospice Journal: Physical, Psychosocial, and
Pastoral Care of the Dying*
c/o Haworth Press
12 West 32nd Street
New York, NY 10001

Illness, Crises and Loss Journal
c/o Charles Press
P.O. Box 15715
Philadelphia, PA 19103

Omega—The Journal of Death and Dying
c/o Baywood Publishing Company
26 Austin Avenue
Amityville, NY 11701
(800) 638-7819

Suicide and Life-Threatening Behavior
c/o Guilford Press
72 Spring Street
New York, NY 10012

Thanatos
P.O. Box 6009
Tallahassee, FL 32314

The Thanatology Newsletter
c/o Health & Nutrition Sciences
Brooklyn College
Brooklyn, NY 11210-2889
(718) 951-5553

World Wide Web Sites

An Internet "Garden of Remembrance" has been opened on an Internet World Wide Web site: DeathNET. You can place a memorial on the site and it will be displayed according to your wishes. What you are doing is depositing a creative imprint of the dead person in the global memory of the future. You can design any message you wish, with photos of the person, sequences from home videos, and tributes from friends. You can update it or change it as often as you wish. The Internet address is: <http://www.islandnet.com/deathnet/garden.html>

Bereavement and Hospice Support Netline: www.ubalt.edu/bereave-ment

DeathNET
http://www.rights.org/
deathnet/open.html
Serves as an international archive specializing in all aspects of death and dying including DeathTALK, ERGO! Information Center, Garden of Remembrance, Human Rights Campaigns, The Living Will Center, Media Monitor, Student Research Center and more.

Death and Dying includes references for probate, wills, living wills, and powers of attorney: www.death-dying.com

Estate and Funeral Planning
http://www.ice.net/
kstevens/ELDERWEB.HTM
Offers information and resources for estate and funeral planning, death notices and obituaries, eulogies and elegies, prayers for the departed, and dealing with bereavement. Estate planning links to information on safe deposit boxes, nursing home planning, pre-planned funerals, death benefits, life insurance, and books of interest.

Internet Cremation Society: www.cremation.com

Internet Resources on Aging and Loss
gopher://gopher.rivendell.org/11/resources/aging
Central listing of information for elderly persons coping with death and dying.

National Funeral Directors Association: www.nfda.com

Sociology of Death
http://www.interport.net
mkearl.death.html
A key Web site for accessing important information on the sociology of death, including: general resources; death across cultures and time; symbolic immortality and longevity; death and social institutions, political economics, medicine, and religion; moral debates; and personal impacts of death.

Virtual Memorial Gardens
http://catless.ncl.ac.uk/obituary/memorial.html
http://www.dgsys.com/~tgolden/1grief.html
websites honoring deceased persons and pets

Counseling

If you find it difficult to struggle with grief's stages, seek the support of a counselor. In the darkness of despair, you might forget that there really are others who care for you if you will let them. You may not want others to see you upset. If you show the magnitude of your loss to those close to you, you fear you will bring them pain as they see you suffer. So you might tend to isolate yourself, seeking to conceal your grief. It is not a sign of weakness as some think, but a wise sign of strength and character. Counseling provides growth—greater strength and understanding and a deeper healing.

> If I am a good listener, I don't interrupt the other nor plan my own next speech while pretending to be listening. I try to hear what is said, but I listen just as hard for what is not said and for what is said between the lines. I am not in a hurry, for there is no pre-appointed destination for the conversation. There is no need to get there, for we are already here; and in this present I am able to be fully present to the one who speaks. The speaker is not an object to be categorized or manipulated, but a subject whose life situation is enough like my own that I can understand it in spite of the differences between us. If I am a good listener, what we have in common will seem more important than what we have in conflict (Westphal, 1984, p. 12).

PART FOUR

Therapeutic Guidelines

CHAPTER 4

Interventions and Activities

To laugh is to risk appearing the fool.
To weep is to risk appearing sentimental.
To reach to another is to risk involvement.
To expose your feelings is to risk exposing your true self.
To place your ideas, your dreams before a crowd is to risk their loss.
To love is to risk not being loved in return.
To live is to risk dying.
To believe is to risk despair.
To try is to risk failure.
But risks must be taken, because the great hazard in life is to risk nothing;
They may avoid suffering and sorrow, but they cannot learn, feel, change, grow, love, live.
Chained by their attitudes they are slaves.
They have forfeited their freedom.
Only a person who risks is free.

—Author Unknown

For the past twenty-five years health care professionals have shown an increased interest in the field of death and dying. In the 1970s when we began consulting, teaching, and treating, very little information was available to guide professionals. Since that time, much has been written to advance our understanding of the grief process, but less has been done on therapeutic intervention with those who are grieving.

Most of us can identify with the feelings that inspired George Bernard Shaw to write the words, "The helper in us all." We feel a sense of purpose in our work. Helping others expresses our own values and personal goals allows us to make a positive difference in the world.

Dying is a time when people need help. They need help with daily living. They need emotional support. We cannot take the problem away, but we can certainly lighten the load and make it more bearable.

As much as we want to help during a time of dying, our behavior may not match our intention. What do we say? What do we do? What is helpful and what is not? How can we tell the difference?

Counseling, like education, can occur under informal circumstances or as part of a structured therapeutic program. The boundary between counseling and education can be crossed with ease from one side to the other. A teacher may have a classroom discussion that transforms into a personal sharing session that gives advice to a student on a death-related topic. A funeral director may be able to reduce anxiety by providing information regarding legal matters before and after a death.

> Humankind will survive only through the commitment and involvement of individuals in their own and others' growth and development as human beings. This means development of loving and caring relationships in which all members are as committed to the growth and happiness of the others as they are to their own. Through commitment to personal growth individual human beings will also make their contribution to the growth and development—the evolution—of the whole species to become all that humankind can and is meant to be. Death is the key to that evolution. For only when we understand the real meaning of death to human existence will we have the courage to become what we are destined to be (Kübler-Ross, 1975, p. 165).

This portion of the book is aimed at helping mental health practitioners to better understand all areas of grief in order to help those who are grieving and dying.

In my practice as a counselor, I occasionally run a bereavement therapy group. From the beginning of my first group experience, I felt as though I had been given a special gift. People share their ideas, secrets, disappointments, horrors, and memories. Many times, after bonding occurs, they disclose to the group private things they have never shared with anyone else. I have tremendous respect for them. It takes courage to look inside and examine oneself. My own life has taught me that this personal exploration can lead to a fuller, happier future. It is my personal journey through grief that brought me to my work as a counselor. My goal in helping someone with their grief is this: try and lessen their pain by reminding them that as long as they have sweet memories, the spirit of their loved one will never die.

In this chapter I want to discuss what a therapy group is and what it has to offer someone who is grieving. I also provide you with exercises that can be helpful in confronting your grief.

Death is still a very personal and unique event. As for caregivers, we need to keep these thoughts in mind as we find the best approach for a particular client and/or family.

> You cannot discover new oceans, unless you have the courage to lose sight of the shore.
>
> — Author Unknown

GROUP TYPES

First, let me draw a distinction between the kinds of groups available to one who is bereaved—self-help or support groups, counseling groups, and what I perceive to be a more intense implement of change—the therapy group.

All three groups have similar characteristics, but differ primarily by the manner in which members interact and the presence and style of group leadership.

Self-Help Groups

Self-help groups, while focused on grieving, are usually centered around a common theme—widowhood, death of a child, suicide, etc. They are designed to

- assist in helping with the sense of isolation felt
- provide education about the group process
- validate the reactions of participants
- help with building new relationships
- provide reassurance that mourners will eventually resolve their grief

While this is done mainly with the support of others in the group, the members are not obligated to participate or even to attend on a regular basis.

Counseling Groups

Counseling groups, as opposed to therapy groups, provide assistance for the bereaved moving through the process as expected—that is, uncomplicated bereavement. There is a designated leader and more structure than the self-help format.

Although leaders have training, this experience varies widely from trained volunteers to professionals with advanced degrees. Counseling groups include some of the components found in both self-help groups and therapy groups, depending on the leader's ability and treatment philosophy.

Therapy Groups

The therapy group provides a forum for those who are having more than the usual difficulty in resolving their grief—most often as a result of personal issues other than the grief itself. All of the factors found in the self-help group and counseling group also apply to the therapy group; however, there are three additional elements that are unique to the therapy group:

- a focus on recapitulating the primary family in terms of similar behavior within the group
- special consideration given to interpersonal learning and socialization techniques
- the challenge of working through existential issues

As a bereavement counselor, I have found it very important for members to come to terms with their own mortality before they can successfully work through the grief process; therefore, I have added an educational component to my bereavement program.

Unlike a self-help group, a therapy group has a designated leader who is usually a mental health professional. I believe the influence and skill I have as a mental health counselor allows me to stimulate a powerful interaction which fosters growth within the participants. Rather than dwelling on loss, pain, or emotional catharsis, the group members concentrate on growth, self-knowledge, and existential responsibility.

Effectiveness of Group Therapy

A question many people ask is, "Does grief counseling work?" Colin Parkes (1980) reviewed a number of research studies in an attempt to answer this particular question. He looked at professional services offering support to the bereaved as well as volunteer peer group support. He concluded,

> The evidence presented here suggests that professional services and professionally-supported voluntary and self-help services are capable of reducing the risk of psychiatric and psychosomatic disorders resulting from bereavement. Services are more beneficial among bereaved people who perceive their families as unsupportive or who, for other reasons, are thought to be at special risk (p. 3).

Parkes (1972) conducted the Harvard Bereavement Study and found that one of the difficulties in comparing studies is that they have focused on people from varying age groups, geographical areas, and socioeconomic strata. However, most of these studies do show that the bereaved suffered from more depressive symptoms during the first year after the loss.

After doing some research of my own, I found the most popular group to be the self-help group because no professional is involved. It begins with a group of people who are suffering—usually from the same kind of loss. They are basically a support group for those who need to talk to others who are experiencing the same feelings. Counseling groups and therapy groups are not as popular because most professionals do not have the time to organize and run a group unless, of course, bereavement counseling is their specialty area. Even when professionals do find the time to conduct such a group, they charge high fees because of their expertise which, in the long run, is not beneficial for the average client. Many times there is a co-leader (usually another professional) who shares the time and effort in forming such a group. The fee then is even higher to accommodate the co-leader.

Finding a Support Group

Think how difficult it would be to go alone to a self-help group for the first time as a bereaved person. The bereaved might wonder: Will the group welcome me or alienate me? Will it be morbid? Will it help me or hinder me? What if I break down and cry? What if I can't physically or emotionally drive home? Many people are finding healing in support groups which meet across the country. A support group provides the opportunity for individuals to share with other grieving people the stories behind their grief, and to share the feelings which are a part of mourning. Members not only have the opportunity to work through their own grief experiences, but are encouraged to assist other group members by becoming more caring listeners themselves. Members help one another understand what they are going through (I'm not insane; other people who have lost a child feel the same way). Groups become havens—safe places for the group member, where you will be accepted for who you are and where you are at the time. Remember that for most of us there are few benefits in trying to shortcut our individual grief work. There is no way out. One must go through the grief process in order to heal.

Explore the resources of your community. Reaching out to the suffering is intrinsic to Judeo-Christian belief. It's no coincidence that so many support groups use synagogue and church meeting rooms. Your own rabbi, minister, or priest is a good person to ask for help in finding a group—or put you in contact with someone who has walked in your shoes. Remember, a group does not have to have a national charter to be helpful. Getting together informally with three or four others who are struggling with the same problem can be the beginning of something wonderful. Larger self-help organizations are listed in your local telephone book. My book provides you with a complete list of resources in the section MEANS OF SUPPORT (p. 139). These groups and agencies are there to serve human needs—to help you help yourself. Please don't be afraid to pick up the phone and contact them. They can't help you if you don't ask.

Find a group that makes you feel comfortable. In my own grief, I wandered from group to group because I could not find the right setting for my needs. Ask yourself these questions as you search:

- Does the group contain people you can identify with in terms of age, sex, or life situation? The group does not have to match your needs completely—in fact, the charm of group sharing is the realization that some experiences cross the boundaries of race, class, and age. But if you share nothing of the group's life experience beyond your problem, you may not feel comfortable.

- Does the group contain "survivors"? By survivor, I mean someone who has been coping long enough to give inspiration to others—the widow who laughs as easily as she cries. This does not mean she no longer suffers—only that she is now enjoying life again.

- Does the group give special attention to newcomers? A good group makes it their priority to identify newcomers, to introduce them, and to include them in the conversation.

- Are you comfortable with the structure of the group? Meetings may be scheduled weekly or biweekly, but the frequency of meetings and the duration of the group is set by group members. Some groups are very structured—every meeting follows the same plan. Others have guest speakers share their personal experiences. Some focus on sharing without any plan at all. Avoid workshops that are based on a timetable. They seem to say: "Come to these ten sessions and you will have done the work of grieving." The problem with this type is that it ignores the unique and personal aspect of death. Some people need more than ten sessions. For some, these groups create a new problem—anxiety or guilt that they are not coping as they should be. Don't just join a group. Go to a meeting or two first. Look for a group which is structured to fit your needs.

- Is the leadership appropriate? Support groups are usually demo-cratic in nature—their very reason for being is sharing. A leader who dominates, manipulates, or controls can damage a group's effectiveness. Look for a group with leadership which invites full participation and accepts who and where people are.

When your loved one died, you were surrounded by people—family, friends, neighbors, co-workers, clergy, etc. You could hardly be alone with so many people around you. The passage of time sent them all back to their usual routines and you were left with your daily life—without that one special person who gave meaning and purpose to so much of your life. Your loneliness seems unbearable. It is so easy to get caught up in yourself—to be a martyr and not want to bother anyone. "No one cares about me. They don't come around or call anymore because they have their own lives to lead." It's up to you now. You have to reach out and continue to make overtures to others. This may be as new an experience as the death was. You may never have had to depend on others like you must do now. Never consider yourself a burden. You are not a burden but a blessing. Doing for others is not the only way of being a good person. You can allow others to help you in your need. We all need to be needed. Let others do their share!

Summary

Over the past twenty years health care professionals have shown an increased interest in issues related to death and dying. There has also been an increased interest in the related subject of grief and bereavement. The reason for this is people come to professionals for mental health treatment feeling stuck in their grieving. They come believing that they are not passing through the experience, that mourning is not coming to an end, and that they need help to get through it and get back to living. Also, grief often surfaces as the underlying cause of various physical and mental aberrations. People seek physical and mental health interventions without necessarily recognizing that there may be a grief issue underlying their particular physical or mental condition.

Support groups are good if they are supportive. A supportive group is one that helps you with today and tomorrow and doesn't dwell on the past. A support group should deal with the past death as it affects the present. We can help others and be helped by them. It is nice to know that someone else has had similar experiences. But we need to deal with the present rather than the past. We need to survive holidays, anniversaries, birthdays, and other special days. It helps to know how others have handled these important and difficult times. They can't tell us what to do or not do, but by sharing their own unique feelings, they can, perhaps, be more in touch with our own feelings and needs.

One important goal of a support group is to help the individual to no longer need the group—to assist them in getting on with life and living. It is best when there is someone trained who facilitates such a group, a person who is educated and experienced in counseling. There needs to be someone who can recognize more deep-rooted problems and needs among the group members and make appropriate referrals and suggestions.

> Two animals trading favors each derive an overall advantage. An animal who does not return favors . . . ceases to receive them (Masson, 1995, p. 171).

HEALING ACTIVITIES

The activities provided throughout my program are only one part of the useful elements within the therapy setting. I have chosen the ones that will be most beneficial to you in your grief work. These activities were part of a curriculum in a Death and Dying course I took as part of my undergraduate studies at Suffolk County Community College.

> Every time you heal a part of yourself, you bring more light into the world.
>
> — Author Unknown.

ACTIVITY #1
Fears of Death and Dying

Circle the areas below which generate fear in you.

1. death in general
2. your own death
3. your own dying
4. death of others
5. dying of others
6. death of pet
7. murder
8. suicide
9. cancer
10. heart attack

11. accidents
12. disasters
13. wakes/funerals
14. cemeteries
15. of the unknown

What did you learn by doing this activity?

ACTIVITY #2
Confronting My Own Dying

Circle the phrases which frighten you about your own dying.
1. being alone
2. being a burden
3. losing my intellectual capabilities
4. becoming weak
5. the pain involved
6. being looked down upon
7. being declared dead when I am still alive
8. losing control
9. that my death will not be witnessed
10. being emotionally overwhelmed
11. looking ugly
12. being hooked to machines and other gadgets
13. not knowing what is going on
14. not knowing what will happen
15. being buried alive
16. not receiving adequate medical care
17. dying of cancer
18. isolated from others
19. dying young
20. dying slowly
21. dying violently
22. being too weak to say good-bye to my loved ones
23. dying in a fire
24. drowning
25. being in agony
26. that I might act in a disgraceful manner
27. that I will be murdered
28. suffocating
30. dying from AIDS

ACTIVITY #3 – Part One
Letter of Apology

Write a letter to your loved one. This task is risky and powerful. Recognize that and recognize your support people if you should need them. Its purpose is to confront unspoken feelings. Remember, there is no need to apologize for thoughts or feelings—only behaviors.

ACTIVITY #4 – Part Two
Return Letter

Now that you have written your letter of apology, write another letter to yourself from the deceased person. This person will tell you they forgive you for each behavior you are apologizing for.

ACTIVITY #5
Are You Prepared?

Even after the most tedious matters, your existence continues after your last breath. Responsibility for dealing with your body passes to your next of kin or appointed representative. But if you want to leave behind an atmosphere of genuine support for your loved ones, be clear in advance about what is likely to happen and what your wishes are.

1. Do you have a legal will?

2. Have you acquired a cemetery plot?

3. Is the beneficiary clause on all legal documents up-to-date?

4. Have you discussed your funeral with loved ones?

5. Have you made funeral or crematory arrangements for yourself?

6. Would your family know where to locate important documents?

7. Would your family know what church, funeral home, or official to contact when you die?

8. Do you have plans to donate your organs at the time of death?

ACTIVITY #6
How Would You Wish to be Remembered?

If you were to die tomorrow, how would you wish to be remembered? List five ways.

1.

2.

3.

4.

5.

ACTIVITY #7
Sibling Death

The purpose of this activity is to explore the trauma of the death of a sibling on oneself and the family system. Order the following list of feelings as you experienced them or would probably experience them at the death of a sibling.

depression	guilt	shame	embarrassment
relief	sorrow	fear	anger
loneliness	resentment	glad	responsibility

1. _____   5. _____   9. _____

2. _____   6. _____   10. _____

3. _____   7. _____   11. _____

4. _____   8. _____   12. _____

Compare your answers with those who have experienced the death of a sibling.

1. How much of you died (would die) at the death of a sibling?

2. How much of your family died (or would die)?

3. What role(s) was (were) lost in the family with the death?

ACTIVITY #8
Children and Death

Despite the fact that there are professionals and groups providing support and advice to those affected by the death of a child, there are still questions we can all ask ourselves, whether parents or not, about our own attitude:

1. What assumptions do you make about the extent to which you can protect children from death?

2. What answers would you give to a child who asks you about death and about what will happen when you die and they die?

It should not be considered morbid to dwell on these questions. They can arise at any time, either directly or as a result of disasters or other tragedies reported in the news media. It is one of the greatest acts of love and compassion to examine these realities with an open heart.

ACTIVITY #9
Parent Death

Choose the death of one of your parents (or both, but do them separately) and write down your feelings regarding the following questions:

1. What circumstances led up to this death? Write about the actual event istelf.
2. How did you cope? To whom did you turn to for help?
3. Describe the moment you knew your life had changed as a result of this death.
4. What are your feelings about this death today?

ACTIVITY #10
Pet Death

Write down your feelings about the death of your favorite pet. You can start at the beginning of the relationship—how and where did you get your pet, what you loved best about your pet, and then the death of your pet.

GLOSSARY

As the field of grief counseling has developed, the need to differentiate among the terms once used interchangeably has become more important. This need has grown out of an increasing awareness and understanding of the complexity of the process. It is not simply an exercise in semantics, because the better our understanding, the more effective the interventions we can design to further the healing process.

Anticipatory grief is an experience of grief that occurs prior to the death of a loved one and emanates from the expectation of emotional pain and the life changes the loss will bring. Although it does not completely prepare a survivor for the emotional experience of the actual loss, it does allow time for resolving emotional issues with the deceased and preparing for the future. Sudden death is particularly difficult to handle since, in most cases, it does not allow this process to take place.

Bereavement is the general state of being that results from having experienced a significant loss. It is the most comprehensive description for one who has experienced the death of a loved one because it encompasses a wide range of reactions—emotional, cognitive, spiritual, behavioral, and physical.

Grief refers to the intrapsychic process of regaining equilibrium after a loss and requires reorganization on both emotional and cognitive levels. The manifestations of this include emotional catharsis and obsessive thoughts of the deceased. However, the process of reevaluating spiritual issues and the presence of physical symptoms and behavioral changes also indicate that this intrapsychic process is occurring.

Grief counseling involves helping a grieving person work through their grief process to a healthy completion within a reasonable amount of time.

Grief therapy involves helping a person with abnormal or complicated grief reactions. Grief is considered abnormal or complicated when it is excessive in length and/or never ends in a satisfactory manner. Specialized techniques, such as Gestalt Therapy (talking to an empty chair), role-playing, and relaxation methods are used to help the person who fails to grieve the death of a loved one.

Grief work is the process by which the bereaved comes to terms with the death of a loved one. It is difficult and takes a great deal of emotional and physical energy to restore a sense of balance to one's life. To a significant degree, it requires a new identity and sense of reality.

Hospice means "host" or "guest" in Latin and refers to a comprehensive philosophy of compassionate care for the terminally ill. Hospice provides support and care for a person in the last phases of their illness so they may live as fully and comfortably as possible.

Mourning is the public expression or sharing of the feelings of grief. This usually takes the form of a ritual such as a funeral service or wearing black. The period of mourning can vary significantly by culture, and considerable variation is seen among individuals and families within the same culture.

Resolution of grief is the result of accepting the reality of the loss both cognitively and emotionally and reorganizing the many facets of one's life (personal identity, relationships with others, use of time, meaning of life) to accommodate the absence of the deceased. Thus, it is not a return to "one's old self" because the death of a loved one changes us and our world profoundly and permanently. Resolution is referred to as a "process" because the efforts to adjust never really end and require continuing energy, albeit to varying degrees. The evidence that the major phases of resolution have occurred include the ability to remember the deceased without the intense pain experienced after the death, together with renewed energy and enthusiasm for living and for other relationships, has suggested that the term "reconciliation" is more appropriate to describe this phase of healing, given that we never fully resolve our pain but continue to adjust as time goes on.

Sudden death refers to a death which is unanticipated or unexpected (e.g., heart failure).

Unfinished business are problematic interpersonal issues that may surface later during the grief response. The pain of the loss may overshadow the need to resolve these issues and thus they become more intense (Worden, 1991).

Togetherness

Death is nothing at all I have only slipped away
into the next room.

Whatever we were to each, that we are still.
Call me be my old familiar name, speak to me in the
easy way which you always used.

Laugh as we always laughed at the little jokes
we enjoyed together. Play, smile,
think of me, pray for me.

Let my name be the household word that it always was.
Let it be spoken without effort.

Life means all that it ever meant.
It is the same as it ever was.
There is absolutely unbroken continuity.

Why should I be out of your mind because
I am out of your sight?

I am waiting for you, for an interval somewhere
very near—just around the corner.

All is well. Nothing is lost.

One brief moment and all will be as it was before—
only better, infinitely happier and forever—
we will all, one day, be one together with Christ.

— Author Unknown

Bibliography and Suggested Readings

Angel, Mark D. (1987). *The Orphaned Adult*. New York: Human Sciences Press.

Attig, Thomas (1996). *How We Grieve: Relearning the World*. New York: Oxford University Press.

Banks, R. (1991). *The Sweet Hereafter*. New York: HarperCollins.

Bissell, Charles B. (1983). *Letters I Never Wrote—Conversations I Never Had*. New York: Macmillan.

Bloomfield, Harold (1983). *Making Peace With Your Parents*. New York: Ballantine Books.

Brinkman, June M. and Teresa F. Quarles (1988). *Death Education Resource Book*. Portland, Maine: J. Weston Walch, Publisher.

Brooke, Avery (1975). *Plain Prayers for a Complicated World*. Noroton, Connecticut: Vineyard Books, Inc.

Buscaglia, Leo (1982). *The Fall of Freddie the Leaf*. Thorofare, New Jersey: Slack Incorporated.

Caine, Lynn (1974). *Widow*. New York: Macmillan, Inc.

Colgrove, M. (1981), Harold Bloomfield, and Peter McWilliams. *How to Survive the Loss of a Love*. New York: Bantam Books.

Cook, Alicia Skinner and Daniel S. Dworkin (1992). *Helping the Bereaved*. New York: Basic Books, Inc..

Corr, Charles A., Clyde M. Nabe, and Donna M. Corr (1997). *Death & Dying, Life & Living*. New York: Brooks/Cole.

Coughlin, Ruth (1993). *Grieving: A Love Story*. New York: Random House.

Crenshaw, David A. (1991). *Bereavement: Counseling the Grieving Throughout the Life Cycle*. New York: Continuum Publishing Company.

D'Arcy, Paula (1990). *When Your Friend is Grieving*. Wheaton, Illinois: H. Shaw Publishers.

DeSpelder, L. A. (1996). *The Last Dance: Encountering Death and Dying*. Fourth Edition. California: Mayfield Publishing Company.

Dietz, Bob (1988). *Life After Loss*. Tucson, Arizona: Fisher Books.

DiGiulio, Robert C. (1989). *Beyond Widowhood*. New York: The Free Press.

Doka, Kenneth (1995). *Children Mourning, Mourning Children*. Washington, DC: Hospice Foundation of America.

Doka, Kenneth (ed.) (1996). *Living With Grief After Sudden Loss*. Bristol, Pennsylvania: Taylor & Francis.

Doka, Kenneth, with John Morgan (1993). *Death and Spirituality*. Amityville, New York: Baywood.

Eadie, Betty J. (1992). *Embraced by the Light*. California: Gold Leaf Press.

Feifel, Herman (1959). *The Meaning of Death*. New York: McGraw-Hill Book Co.

Ferrini, Armeda F. and Rebecca L. Ferrini (1989). *Health in the Late Years*. Iowa: Wm. C. Brown Publishers.

Fitzgerald, H. (1994). *The Mourning Handbook: A Complete Guide for the Bereaved*. New York: Simon & Schuster.

Fleming, S. and L. Balmer (1996). Bereavement in Adolescence. In C. A. Corr and D. E. Balk (Eds.). *Handbook of Adolescent Death and Bereavement* (pp. 139-154). New York: Springer.

Frank, A. W. (1991). *At the Will of the Body: Reflections on Illness*. Boston: Houghton Mifflin.

Ginsburg, Genevieve (1995). *Widow: Rebuilding Your Life*. Tucson, Arizona: Fisher Books.

Glick, Ira O., Robert S. Weiss, and C. Murray Parkes (1974). *The First Year of Bereavement*. New York: John Wiley & Sons, Inc..

Grollman, E. (ed.) (1967). *Explaining Death to Children*. Boston: Beacon Press.

Huntley, Theresa (1991). *Helping Children Grieve*. Minneapolis: Augsburg Fortress.

Jung, Carl (1933). *Modern Man in Search of a Soul*. New York: Harcourt.

Kalish, Richard A. (1981) *Death, Grief, and Caring Relationships*. Second Edition. California: Brooks/Cole Publishing Company.

Kastenbaum, Robert J. (1986). *Death, Society, and Human Experience*. Third Edition. Ohio: Charles E. Merrill Publishing Company.

Katafiasz, Karen (1995). *Finding Your Way Through Grief*. St. Meinrad, Indiana: Abbey Press.

Katzenbach, J. (1986). *The Traveler*. New York: Putnam.

Kelly, Orville (1979). Making Today Count, in Larry A. Bugen (Ed.). *Death and Dying: Theory / Research / Practice*. Dubuque, Iowa: William C. Brown.

Kübler-Ross, Elisabeth (1969). *On Death and Dying*. New York: Macmillan.

Kübler-Ross, Elisabeth (1974). *Questions and Answers on Death and Dying*. New York: Macmillan.

Kübler-Ross, Elisabeth (1975). *Death: The Final Stage of Growth*. New Jersey: Prentice-Hall, Inc..

Kübler-Ross, Elisabeth (1981). *Living With Death and Dying*. New York: Macmillan.

Kübler-Ross, Elisabeth (1983). *On Children and Death*. New York: Macmillan.

Kuenning, Delores (1987). *Helping People Through Grief*. Minneapolis, Minnesota: Bethany House Publishers.

Kushner, Harold S. (1983). *When Bad Things Happen to Good People*. New York: Avon Books.

Larson, Dale G. (1993). *The Helper's Journey: Working With People Facing Grief, Loss, and Life-Threatening Illness*. Champaign, Illinois: Research Press.

Lendrum, Susan and Gabrielle Syme (1992). *Gift of Tears: A Practical Approach to Loss and Bereavement Counselling*. New York: Routledge.

Lewis, C. S. (1979). *A Grief Observed*. New York: Bantam Books.

Lifton, R. J. (1977). The Sense of Immortality: On Death and the Continuity of Life. In H. Feifel (Ed.). *New Meanings of Death*. New York: McGraw-Hill.

Lonetto, Richard (1980). *Children's Conceptions of Death*. New York: Springer.

Marcel, G. (1962). *The Philosophy of Existentialism* (2nd Ed.). Trans. M. Harari. New York: Citadel Press.

Markman, Peter T. and Roberta H. Markman (1989). *10 Steps in Writing a Research Paper*. Fourth Edition. New York: Barron's Educational Series.

Masson, J. A. and S. L. McCarthy (1995). *When Elephants Weep: The Emotional Lives of Animals*. New York: Delta/Dell.

May, G. (1992). For They Shall be Comforted. *Shalem News, 16*:2, p. 3.

Montaigne, M. de (1991). *The Essays of Michel de Montaigne*, M. A. Screech (Trans. and Ed.). London: Allen Lane.

Moody, Raymond A. (1975). *Life After Life: The Investigation of a Phenomenon: Survival of Bodily Death*. Atlanta: Mockingbird Books.

Morse, M., D. Castillo, and D. Venecia et al. (1986). Childhood Near-Death Experiences. *American Journal of Diseases of Children, 140*, pp. 1110-1113.

Munson, R. (1993). *Fan Mail*. New York: Dutton.

Nuland, Sherwin B. (1993). *How We Die: Reflections on Life's Final Chapter*. Connecticut: Alfred A. Knopf, Inc.

Parkes, Colin (1972). *Bereavement: Studies of Grief in Adult Life*. New York: International Universities Press.

Parkes, C. and R. Brown (1972). Health After Bereavement: A Controlled Study of Boston Widows and Widowers. *Psychosomatic Medicine, 34*, pp. 449-461.

Rando, Therese A. (1984). *Grief, Dying, and Death: Clinical Interventions for Caregivers*. Champaign, Illinois: Research Press Company.

Raphael, Beverly (1983). *Anatomy of Bereavement*. New York: Basic Books, Inc.

Reoch, Richard (1996). *To Die Well*. New York: HarperCollins.

Rinpoche, Sogyal (1994). *The Tibetan Book of Living and Dying*. San Francisco, California: HarperCollins.

Sanders, C. M. (1979-80). A Comparison of Adult Bereavement in the Death of a Spouse, Child and Parent. *Omega, Journal of Death and Dying, 10*:4, pp. 303-321.

Sanders, Catherine M. (1989). *Grief: The Mourning After*. New York: John Wiley & Sons.

Schiff, Harriet Sarnof (1986). *Living Through Mourning*. New York: Viking Penguin, Inc.

Seneca (4 B.C.-65 A.D.). Stoic philosopher.

Shelley, J. A. (ed.) (1982). *The Spiritual Needs of Children.* Downers Grove, Illinois: Intervarsity Press.

Silverman, Phyllis R. (1986). *Widow to Widow.* New York: Springer Publishing Company, Inc.

Silverman, William B. and Kenneth M. Cinnamon (1990). *When Mourning Comes: A Book of Comfort for the Grieving.* Northvale, New Jersey: Jason Aronson Inc.

Singer, Lilly, Margaret Sirot, and Susan Rodd (1988). *Beyond Loss.* New York: E. P. Dutton.

Smilansky, Sara (1987). *On Death: Helping Children Understand and Cope With Death.* New York: Peter Lang Publishing, Inc.

Smyth, P., and D. Bellemare (1988). Spirituality, Pastoral Care, and Religion: The Need for Clear Distinctions. *Journal of Palliative Care, 4*:1&2, pp. 86-88.

Strand, Robert (1996). *Moments for Mothers.* Green Forest, Arkansas: New Leaf Publishing Company.

Tatelbaum, Judy (1984). *The Courage to Grieve: Creative Living, Recovery, and Growth Through Grief.* San Francisco, California: Harper & Row.

Truman, Jill (1987). *Letter to My Husband.* New York: Viking Penguin, Inc.

Viorst, Judith (1987). *Necessary Losses: The Loves, Illusions, Dependencies and Impossible Expectations That All of Us Have to Give Up in Order to Grow.* New York: Fawcett Books.

Wallace, William (1998). *Living Again: A Personal Journey for Surviving the Loss of a Spouse.* Lenexa, Kansas: Addax Publishing Group.

Watts, A. W. (1957). *The Way of Zen.* New York: Pantheon.

Westberg, Granger E. (1962). *Good Grief.* Philadelphia, Pennsylvania: Fortress Press.

Westphal, M. (1984). *God, Guilt, and Death.* Bloomington, Indiana: Indiana University Press.

Williams, Margery (1998). *The Velveteen Rabbit.* New York: Barnes & Noble Books.

Wolfelt, Alan (1983). *Helping Children Cope With Grief.* Indiana: Accelerated Development, Inc.

Worden, J. William (1991). *Grief Counseling & Grief Therapy.* New York: Springer Publishing Company.

Yalom, I. (1980). *Existential Psychotherapy.* New York: Basic Books.

Yancey, Philip (1977). *Where is God When It Hurts?* Grand Rapids, Michigan: Zondervan.

Index

DATE DUE
